FOCUS ON GOD

Focus on God

Frances Young
and Kenneth Wilson

WIPF & STOCK · Eugene, Oregon

Wipf and Stock Publishers
199 W 8th Ave, Suite 3
Eugene, OR 97401

Focus on God
By Young, Frances M. and Wilson, Kenneth
Copyright©1986 Methodist Publishing - Epworth Press
ISBN 13: 978-1-4982-0714-0
Publication date 11/25/2014
Previously published by Epworth Press, 1986

Every effort has been made to trace the current copyright owner of this publication but without success. If you have any information or interest in the copyright, please contact the publishers.

CONTENTS

Preface by John Newton		vii
Foreword		ix
Introduction		1
1	The Implications of Vocation	3
2	Using the Bible as a Theological Resource	17
3	Using the Tradition as a Theological Resource	33
4	Using Science as a Theological Resource	47
5	Using History as a Theological Resource	63
6	Using Literature as a Theological Resource	77
7	Community Wisdom	91
8	Addressing God	105
	Postscript	123
	Suggestions for Further Reading	131

PREFACE

This book is an eloquent plea for Christians, and especially ordained ministers, to love God more fully with their minds. John Wesley was convinced that reason and religion belong together and that 'all irrational religion is false religion'. Frances Young and Kenneth Wilson write from the Methodist tradition, and like Wesley they are extremely practical theologians.

Certainly they are in no sense narrowly academic or intellectualist. Yet they make it crystal clear that the Christian minister's central task of enabling people to discern God involves searching intellectual and theological effort. It embraces spirituality, of course, but it also means wrestling with the reality of God in both thought and practice.

No one can read this book without, I believe, gaining a broader and deeper view of the calling of the Christian minister. As pastor, teacher and preacher, he or she is called to be a 'bridge-person', mediating the riches of the Christian tradition, and of humane learning (including scientific thought) to the people. The minister cannot do it alone, of course. Theology, like science, is a team effort, and part of the satisfying fulness of this book springs from its being a joint production.

The range of studies spanned by the book may sound daunting, since it includes biblical studies, history, spirituality, literature, and scientific thought. Yet everything turns on the point of view, and this, I repeat, is not narrowly intellectualist. I would buttress that claim in three ways. First, both authors approach their task as theologians engaged in practical ministry and pastoral care. Frances Young, for example, has been markedly influenced in her approach to biblical exegesis by her work with the black churches of Birmingham and their narrative theology, in which they know themselves as caught up into the biblical story of the people of God. Secondly, for them, spirituality and theology are two sides of the same coin; 'thinking and praying belong together' and 'everything . . . in this book is relevant to adoration'. Thirdly, while they affirm the importance of critical and historical study of the Bible and the Christian tradition, they are equally clear that critical study alone is not enough. The detached, analytical approach of the Enlightenment cannot do justice to the richness of reality, either in theology or in any other branch of humane learning. With Blake and Coleridge, Newman and Polanyi, they cry out for reason to be warmed and illuminated by the gifts of imagination and intuition, sympathy and insight. Is this unscientific? On the contrary, it is precisely through imaginative constructs and intuitive guesses that the scientist breaks through to new discoveries and understanding.

The book opens up wide and exciting intellectual horizons. It challenges the reader to far more committed thought and prayer. One of E.M. Forster's pithiest aphorisms is germane to its theme: 'Only connect'. It calls for the Christian minister to be a bridge-person between the theologians and the people in the pew, and between the arts and sciences, and the wayfaring Christian. It is a tall order, but remember it is a corporate enterprise. This book has a vital relevance to ministerial training and continuing education. Frances Young and Kenneth Wilson do not merely set before us the challenge and excitement of the task. By the quality of their thought and writing, they begin to demonstrate how it may be fulfilled, to the glory of God and the enrichment of humankind.

Feast of St Francis Xavier
4 December 1985

John A. Newton
West London Mission

FOREWORD

The book has emerged from a shared interest in the primary theological task of the minister. Our complementary experience led to the particular distribution of responsibility for the chapters; thus Frances Young wrote the first three chapters and chapter eight, and Kenneth Wilson chapters four to seven. However, the overall conception and planning has, we believe, given a coherence of theological direction which we have found significant. If the Christian community is to witness to the reality of God's presence in the world, it needs ministers and clergy who accept the daunting but exciting task of theological enquiry: our intention is to stimulate it.

We are both Methodists, as it happens; however, what we write is of relevance to other traditions since the opportunities which we all face depend equally upon our attention to God if they are to be faithfully grasped. In that connection it should be said that although we use the word 'minister' in the text, the word 'priest' can be substituted by any reader.

Frances Young
Kenneth Wilson

Introduction

What is the primary task of ministry? In the last decades there has been an enormous change both in what is expected of a minister, and in what is provided by way of training. The human sciences, psychology and sociology, have been exploited so as to professionalize pastoral care, and the utilitarian values of our society have put pressure on ministers to be seen to be doing something, to become more and more involved in social and community work. Inevitably, increase in one kind of activity means cut-back in others, or else overwork and diversification lead to a loss of focus. This book is written against a background in which the discipline of study and the importance of theology seem less and less at the centre of concern in the churches.

It is not that we dispute the fact that the gospel has practical outworkings, nor that we underestimate the importance of learning from contemporary movements of thought, counselling methods, or social and political analyses. But we do wish to direct attention again to what the minister has which neither social worker nor psychologist necessarily has – in fact may reject – namely a commitment to the reality of God and the possibility of knowing God. We also want to recall people to a sense of the need for vision, for a wider perspective than immediate slogans and fashions, for reflection and serious enquiry, if anything we do is to contribute responsibly to a better future. Theology is not an optional extra, but the heart of the matter.

In the course of this book we wish to commend again areas of study which have become problematic for the life of the Church, or have begun to seem irrelevant. This does not mean we are insensitive to the importance of many areas we do not discuss here – simply that we are concerned about the diminishing respect for those we do. The traditional theological disciplines – biblical study and history of doctrine, while still given recognition, are often felt to complicate the minister's task rather than help; it is all too easy to abandon, or to refuse to struggle with, critical approaches that only seem to undermine the faith, and fall back onto a few simplistic ideas and a limited number of congenial texts and passages of scripture (even the lectionary is restrictive!). Science continues to seem a threat rather than a hand-maid of theology. History does not seem to matter because everything has changed so much. Literature has a dying role in our culture because of the advent of television. In spite of these widespread attitudes, we believe all these things have a positive role to play in enriching our understanding of the world, in informing our efforts to change it creatively and responsibly, and in enabling us to celebrate it as the world God creates and loves. None of them is for the specialist and the specialist alone.

We are not unmoved by the urgency of cries for justice, or the anguish and clamour arising from the poor and oppressed. We respect the voice of the prophets. But the voice of wisdom is also to be found in the Bible. For the sake of balance it is important to affirm the value of thinking on whatsoever things are good, whatsoever things are true, whatsoever things are lovely and of good report, even if we run the risk of speaking with the tones of the privileged elite. In the end Christianity will stand or fall by its integrity, its commitment to truth, the whole truth and nothing but the truth. And as we shall see, what may seem rather intellectual concerns, will not prove irrelevant to the social, political and economic situation in which we all find ourselves.

Theology was once regarded as the Queen of the Sciences. No one these days can claim to master even one branch of knowledge fully, but it remains true that nothing lies outside the province of the theologian. Everything is to be understood in relation to God, and God is to be understood through everything – for God is the source of all. The task of ministry is enabling people to discern God. It is a missionary task and a theological task. What we hope to do is to kindle again the sense of single-minded purpose that can integrate all the minister's activities and interests, and enable those with different gifts and insights to enrich one another, as the whole focus is placed upon God and God alone.

1
The Implications of Vocation

It is usually taken for granted that a minister has responded to a sense of vocation when he or she seeks ordination. What are the implications of this? In this chapter, it will be argued that the implications are very considerable, and that in spite of the weakened sense of the word in general parlance, it is precisely here that the distinctive character of the minister is to be located. The Oxford Dictionary offers as synonyms for vocation, 'employment, trade, profession'; but initially it suggests 'divine call to, or sense of fitness for, career or occupation'. The original connotation of the word was theological. The erosion of the explicitly theological is reflected in the alternative 'sense of fitness for', yet I suppose people who use the word do tend to retain something of the prior sense: if you speak of vocation rather than career, the overtones are those of dedication rather than ambition.

Contrast with that summary of contemporary usage a remark made by Isaiah Campbell, one of the black pastors attending the course run by the Centre for Partnership between Black and White: 'For us, ministry is a vocation, not a profession.' Many of the pastors are employed in factories, hospitals or other secular jobs during the week, and their role as pastor is not the way they earn their living, but a calling which consumes all their spare time. Their position as pastor is dependent upon their ability to describe experiences not dissimilar to those of the Old Testament prophets – Isaiah claims to have seen the same vision as his namesake, described in Isaiah 6.

In Methodism we certainly agree with Isaiah Campbell that ministry begins in vocation. We would not restrict it to the ordained ministry, of course, recognizing that many lay people may have a genuine call from God, and that priesthood belongs to all believers. But not all teachers or social workers or factory workers have a sense of vocation, and many who do would not see it in the explicitly God-centred way that Isaiah sees his pastoral ministry. What distinguishes Christian ministry, whether lay or ordained, is an explicit response to the call of God. That is something that should never be watered down or lost, even if secular techniques are exploited.

As far as the ordained ministry is concerned, the Methodist Church requires that candidates testify to their 'call'. We are less inclined to insist that the call conform to a particular type, allowing a variety of ways in which 'vocation' happens; and our system means that ministry can easily be understood as a profession, and vocation reduced to its popular emasculated meaning. But at heart Methodism accepts the priority of God's call in the making of a minister. Ministry begins there, and the distinctive thing about it lies there.

So what are the implications of this, and what is it a minister is called to do? In order to answer these questions, let us make a careful study of what vocation meant in scripture, not indeed taking on the whole of the Bible in one short chapter, but examining the works of Paul in such a way as to take account of fundamental influences upon him, which include the scriptures we know as the Old Testament.

A rapid survey of a concordance shows that Paul most commonly links 'call' or 'calling' with a person's coming to be a Christian. Thus:

> you are deserting the *one who called you* in the grace of Christ . . . (Gal. 1.6)
>
> This persuasion is not from the one *who calls you* . . . (Gal. 5.8)
>
> . . . *you were called* to freedom, brethren . . . (Gal. 5.13)

All these remarks are addressed to congregations in Galatia. In similar manner, Paul speaks elsewhere of those he addresses as having been called, and clearly refers to their calling as Christians:

> God is faithful, by whom *you were called* into the fellowship of his Son, Jesus Christ our Lord. (I Cor. 1.9)

In I Cor. 7, Paul exhorts his readers to remain in the state in which they were called, whether married, slave, free, etc. So every Christian has a vocation. It is an interesting speculation that the word *ecclesia* (church) which etymologically refers to an assembly 'called out' to a meeting was picked out of the scriptures and used by the Christians to describe their communities precisely because it suggested the notion of being called out of the world into the body of Christ: both *synagoge* (synagogue, a 'gathering together') and *ecclesia* are used of the assembly of God's people Israel in the Septuagint, the Greek Old Testament. Certainly for Paul 'calling' is related to the sheer freedom and sovereignty of God's grace, to God's decision to choose those who have no merit or qualification of their own. In Romans 9, Paul makes it clear that God's purpose of election pre-dates the birth and actions of those he chooses, and depends upon God's *call* rather than on works. He has a hard time defending God from the charge of injustice or arbitrariness (Rom. 9.14 ff.), but clearly links vocation with election to fulfill God's purposes as pre-scribed (i.e. written down in advance) in scripture. For Paul this now means election to the community of the new covenant, and vocation is closely related to justification. This election is something fore-ordained and purposed by God and the initiative rests entirely with God. Unavoidably we face the problems of Rom. 8.28–30:

> We know that in everything God works for good with those who love him, *who are called according to his purpose*. For those whom he foreknew, he also predestined to be conformed to the image of his Son, in order that he might be the first-born among many brethren. And those whom he predestined, *he also called;* and those whom he called, he also justified; and those whom he justified, he also glorified (RSV).

It is true that Paul never draws the logical conclusions from his position which were later to be pressed by Calvin, and it is possible that he did not envisage a predestination of particular individuals but rather the fulfilment in present Christian experience of the intentions pre-dicted (foretold) in the oracles of God; but vocation for Paul is clearly God's prior intention and initiative in summoning human beings to be conformed to the image of his Son. God justifies; God calls. Human beings find themselves chosen to be glorified, and knowing they have no prior claims or qualifications, can only see this as God's pre-determined will.

The great twentieth century theologian, Karl Barth, devotes a sizable portion of the *Church Dogmatics (IV,III.*2) to discussion of 'The Vocation of Man'. Man is called by Christ to an active knowledge of the truth, and thus is received into the new standing of the Christian, namely a particular fellowship with himself; and this propels him into witness and service. Vocation is identified with a person's identity as a Christian which is the result of a prior divine call, and Barth's discussion focuses on the particular event of man's vocation in Christ, its personal character, the dangers of identifying it with psychological states, its relationship with baptism, etc. The goal of vocation is union with Christ, who takes possession of the free human heart, and rules the speech and action of each particular individual. Barth, I suggest, has understood Paul correctly: it is the priority of God's purpose which is fundamental, and this is for every believer a 'vocation to be' a Christian, a member of Christ's body.

On one occasion, however, Paul speaks not of this general vocation of Christians, but of his own personal vocation to be an apostle to the Gentiles:

> . . . he who had set me apart before I was born, and had called me through his grace, was pleased to reveal his Son in me, in order that I might preach him among the Gentiles . . . (Gal. 1.15 RSV)

One interesting thing about this statement is that once again the 'fore-ordaining' of God is fundamental. But now it cannot be domesticated or dismissed as the general fore-ordaining of salvation according to God's plan outlined in scripture; it refers to God's decision in advance that this individual is to carry out some particular task. It seems to me that Romans 8–9, read carefully and in the light of this more personal statement, must carry something of the same force. Romans 9 speaks of the choosing of Abraham, Sarah, Rebecca, Isaac, and emphasizes that this choice was not based on works or merit but on God's call to fulfil a precise role in his plan of salvation. Similarly I suspect that Paul seriously believed that the call of the Christian was not simply to be a member of the community of the new covenant, but also to fulfil a particular role in the history of salvation. Each called individual has some crucial part to play. Nevertheless we can perhaps conveniently generalize by making a distinction between 'called to be a Christian' and 'called to do a specific job'. Paul's own call and commissioning is distinct from that of his converts.

Another feature of what he says in Gal. 1.15 is its background in the prophets, and the more I read Paul, the more convinced I am that one of the most formative influences upon his thinking was a life-long immersion in the scriptures. The most obvious passage is Jer. 1.4 ff.:

> Now the word of the Lord came to me saying,
> Before I formed you in the womb I knew you,
> and before you were born I consecrated you.
> I appointed you a prophet to the nations (RSV).

Here is the precedent for Paul's conviction that God's choice lies behind his very coming to be. The priority of God is fundamental, and in the case of Jeremiah the call of God constantly confronted and overcame his own personal reluctance to get involved at all:

> Then I said, 'Ah Lord God! Behold I do not know how to speak, for I am only a youth.'
> Then . . . the Lord said, 'Behold, I have put my words in your mouth. See I have set you this day over nations and over kingdoms,
> > to pluck up and to break down,
> > to destroy and to overthrow,
> > to build and to plant' (RSV).

Jeremiah's career as a prophet was a tough one, and of all the prophets in the Old Testament, we seem to have the most insight into his personal struggles over his vocation, as he laments and argues with God over what happens to him: he complains against persecution, prays for help and vengeance, pleads his case before God, demands to know why the wicked prosper and why the false prophets get a hearing. In 15.10 ff. for example, Jeremiah utters frantic complaints that his vocation has led him to isolation and persecution, and the only answer he gets is that he has to go on and go on suffering for it. Perhaps the climax of the prophet's protests is to be found in chapter 20.14 ff.:

> Cursed be the day on which I was born!
> The day when my mother bore me, let it not be blessed!

Cursed be the man who brought the news to my father,
'A son is born to you', making him glad.

Why did I come forth from the womb to see toil and sorrow and spend my days in shame? (RSV)

His curse, his despair, picks up the knowledge that came to him at his call that he was chosen and designated by God before he was even born. He is trapped in a situation he does not want. Earlier in this lament he complains at the derision which greets his preaching; but if he says, 'I will not mention him or speak any more in his name,' he feels that there is in his heart, as it were, a burning fire shut up in his bones, and he is weary with holding it in and he cannot.

Now Old Testament scholars have noticed that Jeremiah's laments belong to a particular form which is evidenced elsewhere; particularly striking are the parallels in the psalms, especially Ps. 22:

My God, my God, why hast thou forsaken me?

All who see me mock at me,

Yet thou art he who took me from the womb,
Thou didst keep me safe upon my mother's breasts.
Upon thee was I cast from my birth,
and since my mother bore me, though hast been my God (RSV).

Such parallels perhaps temper the older confidence that the personal religious experiences of the individual prophet are for the first time revealed in Jeremiah's laments. Be that as it may, Paul would have taken the text of Jeremiah at its face value, and it is particularly interesting that if we explore carefully what he has to say about his own vocation as an apostle, there is a kind of community of experience even where there are no traceable verbal parallels. Perhaps *because* of Jeremiah's experience, Paul can point to his own sufferings and persecutions as signs of his genuine call to apostleship (II Cor. 4.7 ff.; 11.23 ff.). He can boast of his weakness, because like Jeremiah he is caught up in something bigger than himself. *The priority belongs to God.* He is obliged to speak the word, and the consequences are quite devastating:

We are the aroma of Christ to God among those who are being saved and among those who are perishing, to one a fragrance

The Implications of Vocation 9

from death to death (perhaps, a deadly stench producing death), to the other a fragrance from life to life (II Cor. 2.15–16) (RSV).

Whatever this difficult statement means precisely, it is clear that the effect of Paul's word is to divide people into parties for and against, and it seems there were occasions when Paul felt that like Jeremiah or Elijah, he alone was left and all the world was against him, the one prophet of God. That God was behind him, had called him and sent him was the one conviction which Paul was never able to compromise, even for the peace of the Church about which he cared so much.

It is this conviction about the priority of God which seems to me to be the most fundamental feature of the experience of vocation as depicted in the Bible. We all know lots of pretty stories from the Bible which describe vocation in very concrete and literalizing ways. The classic is the boy Samuel in the temple, hearing a voice calling his name, running to the one other human being around, eventually discerning that this voice was not a human voice. Then there are the stories of Jesus calling his disciples – concrete calling stories which we take as models of the call of the Christian. The problem for most people today is the very concrete character of the stories and the utterly non-concrete, even non-existent, sense of 'call' in their own experience. So it is easy to get side-tracked into discussions about the character and validity of religious experiences, to note the prevalence of visual and auditory experiences in particular cultures and their absence in others, to speak of psychological states, induced conversion-experiences, or of imaginative identification with stories in such a way that utterly different experiences are assimilated to the alien patterns of the Biblical narratives. Thus may the fundamental event of vocation be reduced through description and analysis. Thus may attention be turned from the fact of God's priority to a person's sense of fitness for the job in hand, the particular personal gifts of the individual which suit the minister for performing a particular function. But this will not do. It is a fact that a vocation often comes to awareness through religious experience of one sort or another – I could myself speak of a 'Damascus Road' experience and an 'Aldersgate Street'; but I think it is significant that Paul never himself describes what happened on the Damascus Road. The blinding light recorded in the book of Acts, whether or not it actually happened that way, was not for him the significant thing. Let us look again at what he says himself about his vocation:

> For I would have you know, brethren, that the gospel which was preached by me is not man's gospel. For I did not receive it from man, nor was I taught it, but it came through a revelation of Jesus Christ. For you have heard of my former life in Judaism, how I persecuted the Church of God violently and tried to destroy it; and I advanced in Judaism beyond many of my own age among my people, so extremely zealous was I for the traditions of my fathers. But when he who had set me apart before I was born and had called me through his grace was pleased to reveal his Son in me in order that I might preach him among the Gentiles, I did not confer with flesh and blood, nor did I go up to Jerusalem to those who were apostles before me (Gal. 1.11 ff. RSV).

Paul's so-called conversion-experience was not merely a move from Judaism to Christianity – a rather anachronistic way of putting it anyway – but a vocation to preach the Gospel which had long-term consequences for the whole of his life and was entirely grounded in his sense of *the priority of God*.

I have suggested that we may make a kind of distinction between a 'vocation to be' and a 'vocation to do' in Paul. All are called to be in fellowship with Christ; Paul and certain chosen individuals are called to *do* certain things as ministers of the gospel and preachers of the word – their calling is more like that of the Old Testament prophets. Yet this distinction cannot be pressed; because being in Christ will have consequences for what a person does, and what a person does inevitably affects what he is. Furthermore, neither Paul nor his converts thought of their vocation as a profession – Paul earned his living by tent-making and encouraged his converts to continue in the state in which they were called and to work for their living as they waited for the end to come in God's good time. What seems to me to be significant is that both types of vocation (insofar as they are at all distinguishable) are grounded in the same prior activity of God, and both are traced back to his pre-determinate will and purpose. I believe Barth has got Paul right and that this is characteristic of an authentic Christian vocation – a sense (by which I mean both an intellectual grasp and a feeling) that one has been placed in a particular position rather than that one has chosen it oneself, a sense that one has been *given* a particular job to do, a sense that somehow the course of one's life has not been fortuitous but that an unseen hand has been shaping it, and that therefore it is possible to submit to and trust that providential guidance for the future without reserve; as the Methodist Covenant-service puts it:

> I am no longer my own, but thine. Put me to what thou wilt, rank me with whom thou wilt; put me to doing, put me to suffering; let me be employed for thee or laid aside for thee, exalted for thee or brought low for thee; let me be full, let me be empty; let me have all things, let me have nothing; I freely and heartily yield all things to thy pleasure and disposal.

Now if this understanding of vocation is along the right lines, then it has certain very important consequences. In the first place, it puts a premium on the priority of God, so alerting us to the fact that how we understand and proclaim the God who has called us is our primary concern as ministers. In the second place, it raises certain classic theological problems, so reminding us that wrestling with theological debates is an inescapable consequence of our vocation. To turn to the second point first: Methodists are by tradition Arminian in their theology and will have no truck with any doctrine of predestination. But to accord this kind of priority to God virtually implies predestination. How are we to maintain any coherence between our experience of vocation and our understanding of universal salvation? It is all very well speaking of grace and election rather than predestination; thus at least we seem to preserve some role for the free response of the individual. But the strong doctrine of God's priority and sovereignty on which this understanding of vocation rests led Paul and Augustine to a view which implicitly if not explicitly accepted predestination. It is all very well reducing the doctrine of providence to the general benevolence of the one who has created and preserved the universe, but that minimalizing doctrine of providence cannot do justice to the scandals of particularity that the Christian tradition has affirmed: how odd of God to choose the Jews, or Paul, or me! The sting of predestination may be drawn by insisting that it is for responsibility, for witness, for martyrdom, *not privilege*, and there are good biblical grounds for that, not least in the epistles of Paul. But on the other hand, to follow Paul and Augustine and Calvin will be to turn Christianity into a kind of fatalism if we are not very careful, and to think of God as arbitrary is inconsistent with affirming his love and faithfulness. The problem of evil and sin, the necessity of maintaining human moral freedom and autonomy for there to be any moral order at all, and many other issues, tell against a strong doctrine of divine providence and election and vocation. How then are we to give an account of what has happened to particular individuals? At least we must do justice to that sense of being caught up willy-nilly in something bigger than ourselves, perhaps unwillingly like Jeremiah, or unexpectedly like Paul. The experience of vocation demands that God's priority be acknowledged somehow, and there is no easy solution. Glib, simplistic or reductionist solutions are unsatisfactory. Theological thinking is vital, both for the Christian who is called to be a Christian (unlike neighbours) and for the minister who is called to be a minister (unlike fellow-Christians).

And if there are theoretical problems, how much more are there existential questions: how does a person, or the church for that matter, distinguish between the authentic call and the counterfeit call? Delusive experiences have led some into mental hospitals. False prophets have enticed people into terrible acts with their claims to divine revelation. Why should we trust Paul's claims? After all, his Corinthian converts were not very happy about them, not to mention the Galatians, the church at Jerusalem, and his many enemies within and without the church. How can we trust our own experience or conviction of vocation? As we tell of it or work it out, we shape it in our own way. We create our own 'myth' and we begin to wonder what the original authentic experience was, whether there was such a thing, whether it was all a figment of the imagination, whether we worked ourselves up into it. All one can say is that 'by their fruits, you shall know them'. The same kind of questions faced the New Testament church, and in a number of places we find attempts to provide criteria, proof. Several attempts are made in John's gospel to validate the claims found on the lips of Jesus himself. And what comes over from the gospels and the epistles is the fact that there is no proof. There are self-authenticating signs which may be recognized by those who have eyes to see and ears to hear, but for those who do not, the Spirit of God appears as an evil spirit with the power of Beelzebub and they unwittingly commit the unforgivable sin. To avoid that takes the gift of discernment, and discernment depends upon knowing the sort of signs to look for, having theological insight. Vocation can only be spoken of 'from faith to faith', and it can only be confirmed in the doing. A risk has to be taken. It is like marriage: you cannot be sure it is going to work; you cannot go into it conditionally because it certainly will not work on those terms; you just have to make a commitment in faith and prove it in the being and doing involved in that commitment. There is a risk – there is a risk in the commitment of Christian faith and in responding to God's vocation, and the validity of the vocation is only discovered in its outworking, its fruits.

Now it may be that this insight is a clue which helps to ease the theoretical problems, at least in part. God's priority must be maintained, and the person's sense of being caught up in something bigger; yet God's respect for a person is such that he can only work out his purposes through the willing co-operation of the person called, he can only call through the particular medium of a person's culture, psychological make-up, social situation, etc. And the call is only confirmed as that person enters into the activity of exploring what God's call means, seeking ways of working it out. Yet the call is betrayed if this becomes a search for self-fulfilment or an effort to perform good works. Only as the person submits himself or herself more and more fully to the prior will and purpose of God does the vocation of God bear fruit.

So what fruit might be expected to validate the particular call of a minister? What is the task to which a minister is called? Earlier I suggested that the very idea of vocation puts a premium upon the priority of God, and that this alerts us to the fact that how we understand and proclaim the God who has called us is our primary concern as ministers. There is, of course, a great deal of truth in the understanding of ministry as primarily pastoral; but if we are not careful that will dislodge the priority of God. Pastoral care is now offered by counsellors and social workers in a purely secular way; what is distinctive about the pastoral care of a minister? Surely it must be his ability to bring the reality of God to bear upon that particular situation. Unless God and the mediation of his grace and love, his judgment and will, is kept at the centre, ministry is reduced to something less than itself. And that means that the pastoral model of ministry is less than adequate, because it too easily suggests a purely emergency service, patching things up when they go wrong. A ministry grounded in God will be primarily concerned with fostering a sense of God's reality in the midst of the whole of life and celebrating it. Praise and thanksgiving, submission and obedience, joy and love and fellowship will be predominant. Of course this also implies that weeping with those who weep has a place alongside rejoicing with those who do rejoice. Petition and intercession, words of comfort and salvation and healing, being with people in the depths of their pain and suffering and despair, all these are also part of ministry. But celebrating the reality and being of God embraces everything, and this will only happen as people's minds and imaginations are fired by God, his love, his beauty, his presence. To effect this demands of the minister that he be a theological resource person at the local level, knowing and communicating the treasures of the faith passed down over many generations, fostering reflection and questioning and the search for ways of discerning God in the present, giving people the bread of life not only at the communion rail, but through the word of preaching, through faithful teaching – not indeed acting as an authority, but as one who like Socrates may be a 'midwife' stimulating the minds of others to think thoughts they had no idea they were capable of. In other words, a minister has a maieutic educational role.

Now it would be possible to argue that this function is the proper apostolic function and that it is as they perform this task that ministers are truly in the apostolic succession; but let one text suffice:

> And they devoted themselves to the apostles' teaching and fellowship, to the breaking of bread and the prayers (Acts 2.42 RSV).

There is no concentration here on rescuing the casualties of life, important though that is. Counselling, social work, pastoral care, administration, all are appropriate functions which have devolved upon the minister as the church now operates. But the heart of it all is teaching, sharing, praying – so building up the community

The Implications of Vocation

in its awareness of God's priority and God's purpose. The role of a minister, it is often said, is that of a 'representative person', not displacing the community of priests to which all the faithful belong, yet embodying in an outwardly visible way the God-focus of the community. The communication of God's word, the mediation of God's love, the realization of God's presence in particular situations is a task to which all Christians are called – yet these tasks are entrusted in a particular way to the minister, the representative person. These are the minister's primary functions, and they imply putting theology and prayer firmly into the centre of a minister's training and life. The minister must beware of trying to be a jack-of-all-trades, and put on the apostolic mantle, rediscovering the proper ministerial role as the theologian of the local church community, passing on the tradition of the faith and nurturing its adaptation in a creative way to the ever-changing situation of the present time. That is what is implied by the very call of God which made the person a minister.

2

Using the Bible as a Theological Resource

The source of the tradition we pass on is the Bible. At one time it would hardly have been necessary to make explicit the place of the Bible as the foundation-document of our faith. But now the Bible has become a source of contention, and its contribution to contemporary Christian life and belief has become problematic, an area of embarrassment or of dogmatism. It is a tragedy that the last 150 years have seen the Protestant Churches divided about the Bible. It is essential that the minister puts biblical study at the centre of all that is done. But how? Many find themselves at a loss, or unable to do anything but fall back on traditional patterns. Let us begin by an attempt to outline the present situation, and then see if some constructive suggestions can emerge.

Few of us know the Bible as it used to be known, few even of those who purport to respect it. Use of the Bible is restricted to well-known and well-loved passages, and many debates on church policy or current issues proceed with general reference to Christian principles rather than by appeal to scripture. No doubt this is to some extent a healthy reaction against the old 'text-slinging' approach to biblical proof, but it also reflects a certain uncomfortable feeling that the Bible is not directly relevant to the complexity of our problems, political, moral, social – even religious. It seems to belong to a world we no longer share. Our situation is so complex that the old biblical ways no longer fit. All of us would no doubt take a biblical text as the normal starting-point of our preaching and see that in a service of worship one or two lessons are read from scripture. The Bible still has its place at the centre of our church life, whatever the tradition to which we belong. Yet so often preaching and thinking is not biblical – instead it leans over backwards to be 'relevant'. Illustrations are drawn from anywhere but the Bible. The Bible is not felt to be alive. Is it any wonder that there are those who have come to understand their vocation to be a defence of the Bible? Those who regard such an endeavour as a dogmatic rearguard action on the part of a naive and narrow group should at least listen to the seriousness of the challenge. The place of the Bible in the church is under threat.

Why should this be so? It is partly that there is such a tremendous output of literature these days that the Bible has become one among many books rather than the only book ever opened, as it was for many of our forebears. It is partly that other means of communication are progressively rendering books obsolete for a sizable proportion of the population – the slogans and pictures of the mass media reduce the ability to concentrate on reading anything that is not immediately clear and gripping. But there are deeper problems than that. The fact is that the Bible, even in a modern translation, is seen as old-fashioned, boring, and not immediately accessible or obviously relevant even to one accustomed to reading. The style of novels has turned the biblical narratives into bare undeveloped episodes without development of character or dramatic tension. Genealogies are dull, miracle-stories are fantastic and the denunciations of a prophet or the arguments of a Paul incomprehensible if not distasteful. Indeed, the commonsense of our culture has devalued and called in question much of what the Bible says.

To add to these difficulties, biblical criticism, justifiably or not, has had a disabling rather than liberating effect upon many who have faced its challenge. It has seemed to involve such a radical placing of the Bible in its historical context that it has become an object of archaeological study divorced from the present. It has seemed to shatter the unity and coherence of the Bible, obscuring its message. It has seemed to make the whole business of using the Bible too academic, and by placing the Bible in the specialist's study to sap people's confidence in their ability to handle it. It has seemed to create an atmosphere of suspicion, rather than facilitate the appropriation of the Bible in the modern world. Often the minister is caught half way between the specialist and the ignorant

Using the Bible as a Theological Resource 19

and feels incapable of communicating between two apparently unrelated worlds. But approached in the right way, proper reading of the Bible is facilitated by the kind of thing that is the concern of background study and criticism. There are things that are incomprehensible without knowledge of the past. There are things that appear contradictory. The Bible cannot be read as a flat, timeless document which appeared out of heaven divorced from the history through which it was formed. If the minister is to be the theological resource person at the local level, it is vital that he or she learn again how to read the Bible so as to live in it, able to discern God's word in it, relate it to the present situation, and facilitate the same experience in the congregation.

'Living within the Bible' is what past generations of the faithful have done, one way or another. One reason why the historico-critical approach has seemed disabling is precisely the fact that it systematically prevents us reading ourselves and our concerns into the text; for that is eisegesis (reading in), not exegesis (reading out). So we are distanced from what makes the text come alive – what makes possible that living within the Bible. But then the fundamentalist reaction has the same effect – for reaction it is. It is no simple return to a pre-critical innocence. For both sides, concern about the relationship of the biblical text to events of the past has been over-dominant. Exactly what happened, its precise reconstruction, exactly how and by whom the accounts were written, exactly what the background of thought and culture was – these are the questions which have been one of the prime concerns of biblical study. So an importance was given to the history behind the text, rather than the text itself, which no one would have considered giving to it until about two hundred years ago. Confirmation of scripture has been sought from archaeology rather than prayer and action, and we have forgotten the long-standing Christian belief that you need the Spirit to read the scriptures. So a bifurcation has taken place – a split between those who would defend the facticity of every biblical statement in these historical terms, and those who find themselves unable to grant that kind of inerrancy. Only recently have we begun to see how damaging this exclusive focus on history has been. It is this which prevents people living in the Bible, for all the time the need to question or justify its more awkward statements distracts from reading it so as to hear what it says. The Bible has for too long been 'in the dock', subject to our interrogation or apologetic, unable to speak for itself in its own way.

What would it mean to allow the Bible to speak in its own way? In fact one of the things that critical study helps us to see is that, if we attend to it, the Bible speaks in many ways, and it is not appropriate to interpret every text by the same methods. Sometimes the Bible invites us to pray, sometimes it instructs, sometimes it tells stories; sometimes it chides, sometimes it rejoices. It is not in fact straightforwardly a history textbook any more than a physics textbook – indeed even those sections which do happen to be historical overlap and re-tell the same stories in more than one way. The stories told of the past are not concerned with the past for its own sake, but rather point to the present or the future, because they give people identity or hope. In other words, the Bible interprets events and actions and makes them relevant to those it addresses, and it encourages its interpreters to engage in the on-going discernment of God's will and purpose in their own history and their own lives, by matching them up, finding analogies, to the events and lives of which stories are told in its pages. Consciously or unconsciously those who live in the Bible are engaged in that kind of interpretative process.

The simplest level of interpretation is the re-telling of a story with the expectation that it is in some way paradigmatic or exemplary. That is what Sunday school teachers have always done, sometimes pointing the moral but not necessarily doing so. Whatever its origin, the tale of Abraham's sacrifice of Isaac says more about self-denial and total trust in God than a doctrinal exposition ever could. No one imagines, surely, that it will be taken as an example to be literally followed, any more than most of us take literally Jesus' words that unless one hates father and mother, wife, children, brothers and sisters, and even one's own life, one cannot be a disciple. The story of Abraham is effective because it provides a gripping and extreme example of what it might mean to give up what is most precious for God. It is hardly any wonder that the early church used the story as a paradigm of God's love in giving up his only Son for our sake. If the story of Abraham is offensive, so is the story of the cross. If we avoid being over-sophisticated, that story or indeed any other – like David's triumph over Goliath – can be left to speak for itself.

On the other hand, rather than just re-telling the story, the biblical version can be examined and attention can be focused on the particular way in which the Bible does the telling so as to point up particular features: David justifies his rejection of Saul's armour by appealing to his highly developed but everyday skill with a sling and stones, a skill specifically developed for protecting his flock from marauding beasts, a skill essential to a shepherd boy. Yet he does not herald his triumph as his own, but as the triumph of God, the proof that God is still the God of Israel and her protector. It is almost a parable of what was said earlier about vocation: God is behind it all, even though human action and skill is the medium. Paying attention to the text, drawing attention to elements in it that might have been missed, this is the beginning of the interpretative process; and it is the starting-point of living within the Bible. For it takes the Bible's way of telling stories as the mould for shaping what is going on in one's own life, telling one's own story, discerning the truth about what is happening in the world around us. Any person, trained or untrained, can take the trouble to pay attention to the text and so begin to live in the Bible. That is what happened when the Bible was put in the hands of the people at the Reformation, and it is still what happens across the world when ordinary people take the Bible seriously.

Of course all parts of the Bible do not have the same impact; selectivity is inevitable – for it involves a process of sympathetic and imaginative identification which is bound to work for some people in some places, other people in others, and not everywhere for everyone. It is quite clear that African Christians instinctively make much more of the Bible's sacrifice language than Westerners for whom sacrifice has been foreign to experience for many centuries. Likewise some cultures and some people have a deep interest in ancestors and family trees, and no doubt even the genealogical tables can strike a chord where that is the case. Where this imaginative identification takes place the massive cultural differences between the situation in Israel in Saul's reign and the situation of the reader melt away, and even when observed, they may become secondary and irrelevant to the reader who expects to learn something by reading the Bible. What such a reader expects to acquire is not facts about what may or may not have happened in the distant past, but truths about the human condition, practical wisdom for coping with life, insight into the God-dimension which so easily gets submerged in the day-to-day business of living, a new perspective, the right spectacles for viewing God, the world, oneself. Whether it be story or psalm, prophetic word or proverb, parable or instruction, the expectant reader will discover a mind enlarged, a faith confirmed, a love kindled, and a life increasingly shaped by living in the Bible. It facilitates an intuitive relating of one's own life to what is read. It is this kind of living in the Bible which gives power to the popular liberation-theology of ordinary people in Latin America, the struggle of blacks for justice in South Africa, and the worship of Pentecostal churches. Of course it also gives tenacity to the Afrikaner who identifies himself with the Chosen Race, his nation's Great Trek with the Exodus, and his prosperity with the blessing of God promised to his faithful. This kind of identification with the Bible has a certain ambiguous quality, and critical awareness, an ability to 'test the spirits' is essential. But surely for most of us it is the identification which we desperately need to recapture in all its simplicity. It is not the precise accuracy with which events of the past are recounted which is of over-riding importance; it is the ability of the Bible to continue to shape our thinking, and that depends not on the letter but on the spirit, the ability of the Spirit to stir the imagination and fire the will through the living and active word of God.

This is not, by any means, to imply that biblical scholarship is not valuable. Indeed it is a great aid even to this simple living in the Bible, if it is to be done appropriately. A children's book retelling the story of the Good Samaritan assumes that ministers of religion, that is the Levite and the priest, are the people most likely to know that they ought to stop and help. But that is the exact opposite of the original sense of the narrative. It is a reading into the story of later Christian assumptions about the priorities of religious ministers. In fact the priest and the Levite were fulfilling their religious obligations by passing by on the other side – they thought he was dead, and to touch a corpse would have made them ritually unclean and unable to perform their duties. How much more pointed the story becomes if you realize that simple fact: religion all to easily gets in the way of plain human compassion! The story is now a shrewd observation still worth making whatever the context. This is just one example of how a little historical background knowledge illuminates the real drift of the meaning. Such knowledge should be respected and

Using the Bible as a Theological Resource 23

sought after. It is potentially enriching and it enables us to take the text more seriously. So does every endeavour to gain a deeper awareness of the original, through comparing different translations, noting what commentators say, even learning the original languages if circumstances permit. Indeed to establish the original meaning of a text may make it clear that it cannot be used to back up certain theological or ethical conclusions – in other words it may provide some criterion for 'testing the spirits' and distinguishing between true and false interpretations. The danger of intuitive and imaginative thinking is that it can jump to conclusions and become highly subjective, and disciplined study can provide an important check on this. But sometimes the pursuit of biblical scholarship has misled people into knowing all about the Bible and not knowing the Bible itself. And besides, we should not deceive ourselves into thinking that we can reach back to exactly the original wording and meaning and fix it for ever. We cannot always be sure what the original words were, because they were copied and recopied for 1400 years or so (in the case of the New Testament, much longer in the case of the Old) before printing was invented, and scribes, even professional ones, were not immune from making mistakes. We cannot always be sure how to translate the original words from one language to another – translation is not a mechanical process but an art which inevitably involves understanding and interpretation. We cannot always be sure that we can catch the meaning intended by the prophet, psalmist, apostle or evangelist, for we are not standing there beside him seeing things in the same way as he does, speaking in the same idiom, able to ask him what he means. That is why scholars do not always agree, and there are endless debates about what the original meaning was. But given all these limitations, it is important to engage in the enterprise to the best of our ability. For it does reap worthwhile dividends. New insights are inevitably fostered. Biblical scholarship is an important aid in our endeavour to live imaginatively in the mind of prophet or psalmist, Paul or Christ, and learn of them. It is not irrelevant or otiose, but has a vital role to play in releasing the word from the chains of the past, provided it is employed for that purpose and not to bind the text to the past in tighter and tighter bonds. The purpose of that imaginative living in the past is to enhance the sense of the Bible's contemporaneity.

With the aid of biblical scholarship our living in the Bible should proceed at a different level – perhaps less naively and more richly, though not necessarily more profoundly. There are some who have no elitist educational advantages who are closer to the mind of Christ simply through daily immersion in the scriptures. Yet for all that, surely it is the minister's job to be the local resource person who can bring to bear upon people's reflective use of the Bible the kind of information which will prevent it going off the rails and provide a richer understanding of what is going on in the text. Ministers will not be disabling experts, because they will listen to those who read the Bible for themselves without the aid of specialist knowledge; yet they are in the front line where dialogue should be taking place between a more informed awareness of what scholarship provides and the imaginative exploration of what it means to shape the life of the church or of individuals by living in the Bible.

Careful study of the New Testament soon reveals that imaginative reflection on the scriptures (i.e. basically the Old Testament) was the fundamental way in which the early Christians developed a theology and interpreted what had happened in their recent experience. It was also the way the scriptures became contemporary for them. All these points can be seen exceptionally clearly in the epistle to the Hebrews, though they could be illustrated from elsewhere. The people addressed by the author of Hebrews were apparently in danger of giving up their Christian profession, and the work is punctuated with warnings about the consequences, exhortations to persevere and general encouragement. In one of these sections the author takes a well-known psalm, and just treats the words as directly addressing those to whom he was writing (or perhaps speaking):

> Therefore as the Holy Spirit says, "Today when you hear his voice, do not harden your hearts as in the rebellion, on the day of testing in the wilderness, where your fathers put me to the test and saw my works for forty years. Therefore I was provoked with that generation, and said, 'They always go astray in their hearts; they have not known my ways.' As I swore in my wrath, 'They shall never enter my rest.' " Take care brethren lest there be in any of you an evil unbelieving heart, leading you to fall away from the living God (Heb. 3.7 RSV).

Using the Bible as a Theological Resource   25

This is the simplest way of making the scriptures contemporary – just assume the words apply in a new and different situation in a quite direct manner. The author proceeds to explore this text, first of all taking the historical situation in the wilderness seriously in order to argue that everyone without exception was included, but then to argue that the promise of 'rest' has not really been fulfilled yet, so that the warning applies to the Christians he is at present addressing. The 'rest' is taken to mean not the entry into the promised land, but the coming of the sabbath rest at the end of time. Disobedience prevented God's people entering it; now Christians must beware in case they too through disobedience miss the rest intended for God's people. It is the contemporary situation which fills the text of the psalm with meaning, not the historical events to which the psalm makes reference.

The epistle to the Hebrews develops its understanding of Christ by imaginative pondering on the scriptures, and this is another example of how it was the creative bringing together of present experience and scriptural text which shaped the early church. Psalms which had once referred to the Davidic king and his role become messianic and acquire new significance:

> So also Christ did not exalt himself to be made a high priest, but was appointed by him who said to him, 'Thou art my Son, today I have begotten thee'; as he says in another place, 'Thou art a priest for ever after the order of Melchizadek' (Heb. 5.5 ff. RSV).

The author creates an understanding of Christ's role by relating these psalms to the life and death of Jesus. He develops the idea of his priesthood, which he acknowledges could not be a priesthood according to the normal Jewish pattern, because if he were descended from the Davidic house, Jesus could not also be descended from Levi. But he also delves back to Genesis where the story of Melchizedek was to be found, and, by interpreting Melchizedek's name and office, builds up a picture of a king-priest, who had an eternal existence by virtue of the fact that Genesis tells us nothing about his origin or destiny. It is this kind of kingly priesthood which Christ exercised, claims the author. Neither the scriptures, nor the picture of Jesus is left the same by this imaginative manner of relating the two. Even more fascinating is the process in chapter ten by which the prophetic denunciation of sacrifice in favour of obedience is turned into an affirmation of the efficacy of Christ's sacrifice on the basis of a version of Psalm 40 which seems to have been produced by a scribal error in the Greek translation, and could not possibly be based on the original Hebrew!

What then are we to make of the New Testament's use of scripture? Clearly interpretative methods are being used which would disturb many of us. The original is being treated cavalierly, whether intentionally or unconsciously. The original reference of words quoted is not taken too seriously, and certainly not literally – indeed allegory very quickly enters the field. And this is not just a feature of Hebrews: every time the New Testament takes a prophetic text or a verse from a psalm as a messianic prophecy the same problem arises; and Paul uses allegory in a number of places. Are we then to dismiss as unacceptable the methods of interpretation we find being used in the New Testament? In fact most of us do – those who accept critical methods do not see any reason for not questioning the validity of these exegetical procedures, and those who do not, pride themselves on believing that a biblical text is to be understood literally, which is exactly how the New Testament writers refuse to treat the scriptures of the Old Testament. It is not the letter that counts but the Spirit, affirmed the early Christians.

It is because a strictly historical reading of the Bible has established itself that no one can take seriously what the New Testament writers were doing. Perhaps this should give us pause, and encourage us to ask whether we have become preoccupied with the wrong issues. After all, what about the messianic prophecies? The church has gone on reading the traditional messianic texts in the services of Nine Lessons and Carols, but many are left feeling very uncomfortable since they really have been convinced that a historical reading of the text is proper and that Isaiah, for example, was speaking a message to King Ahaz in chapter seven and not predicting the birth of Christ centuries later. Certainly allowance has to be made for these important insights into the conscious intention of the original prophet; and yet do we have to *exclude* the old tradition, hallowed by Matthew's use of the text, in the process? Clearly we can no longer think in terms of direct prediction, nor would we dare to make doctrined deductions from texts used in this way. Besides, we have to make allowance

Using the Bible as a Theological Resource 27

for the fact that Jews continue to use the same texts without seeing Christ in them. Yet is it not the case that part of the significance of something may well unfold in the light of subsequent discussion or experience? Let us consider for a moment what happens when meaning is discussed in everyday life. Someone says something, the other person fails to understand or takes it in the wrong way. Discussion ensues. In the process it is generally assumed that the original speaker has the right to say what was meant and to exclude meanings not intended. But there are occasions when it may be admitted that what was actually said did not succeed in expressing the meaning intended; or, more particularly, that what was said could mean what the listener imagined and there was more in it than the original speaker at first realized. This is particularly true of poetry, vision or parable, and what are the words of the Old Testament prophets if not poetry, vision or parable, especially when they sing of the hopes surrounding the fulfilment of God's promises. The early Christians re-read the prophets with new insight given by new experience, and what they did cannot be dismissed. For we know in everyday experience how sometimes seemingly uncanny premonitions tease us out of our matter-of-fact awareness. It is entirely plausible to suggest that prophets and psalmists said more than they knew, however one spells out a doctrine of inspiration. Historical reading has freed us from the idea of mechanical predictions; now we need to be freed from the fallacy that a text has one meaning and that that meaning is confined to what the author intended. The original meaning is important, of course, and provides a yardstick for assessing further meanings or applications, but resonances vibrate across the centuries, and the Bible is at least as transcendent as Homer or Shakespeare. Meaning cannot be simply confined to the historical setting, nor even to fulfilment in Christ – for often fulfilment is still not fully realized. The prophets' hope points us all forward, engages our imagination and endeavour, our prayer and action. To enable this to happen, to help people to dream dreams and see visions through the words of the prophets, is to make the Bible contemporary.

It is in poetry, proverb and parable that the dominant historical reading of the Bible so obviously breaks down. Admittedly the images often belong to particular social and cultural contexts; yet we are not so obtuse surely as to be unable to grasp their abiding human significance. 'As the crackling of thorns under a pot, so is the laughter of fools' (Eccles. 7.6): you do not need to be a nomad in the desert round a campfire to savour a saying like that. Nor is it impossible, whatever some say, for children in the inner city to understand about shepherds and sheep – they grow up with pictures in books and on television, and to visit a farm park or nature centre is fun precisely because a familiar thing in the imagination becomes real. People's understanding is not restricted to their immediate environment or experience – indeed most people appreciate being stimulated to widen their environment and experience by using their imagination. The biblical parables and proverbs do still have a life of their own. To spell out the meaning of poetry, proverb or parable, or to translate it into another cultural idiom is often to narrow its possible resonances or even ruin it – like explaining a joke! There is an imaginative grasp which alone gets the point, and the image is self-authenticating. More extended reflection on a parable or proverb may reveal more potential, and sensitive exposition may unfold this for others, but crass exegesis simply impoverishes.

Indeed, the history of parable-interpretation is instructive. The early church tended to allegorize parables, seeking detailed correspondences between elements in the parable and some higher realm of truth. We see this happening already in the gospels, as in Mark 4, where a detailed exposition of the parable of the sower is spelled out. Another much quoted example is Augustine's treatment of the good Samaritan: the man going down from Jerusalem to Jericho is Adam; Jerusalem is the heavenly city, Jericho signifies our mortality; the thieves are the devil and his angels, who stripped man of his immortality, beat him by persuading him to sin, and left him half-dead, for his life-giving knowledge of God was impaired by sin; the priest and Levite signify the priesthood and ministry of the Old Testament which profit nothing for salvation; and the Good Samaritan is Jesus Christ our Lord. And so it goes on – the inn being the church, the innkeeper St Paul, etc. In modern times there has been a tremendous reaction against this kind of thing. Such detailed correspondences seem to detract from the thrust of the parable, and even if they began with a suggestive and imaginative idea, like seeing the Good Samaritan as a model of Christ, it seems worked to death and killed in the process. Modern approaches to the parables arose from reaction against this: parables were supposed to have only one point, they were supposed to have been generated by crises, particular confrontations, in the ministry of Jesus – all generalizing applications were to be taken as secondary. However, it is gradually dawning on people that this is an inadequate approach. Parables in Jesus' day were often deliberately enigmatic or riddling and they did have more than one point – indeed they were often allegories. Besides, parables of their very nature depend upon the imaginative response of the hearer: their ambiguities, like the ambiguity of poetry, depend upon seeing one thing in terms of another and inviting others to engage in the same imaginative act, opening themselves to its potential surprises. Parables have a life of their own, and it is ridiculous to confine them to precise historical situations even if such particular moments did originally generate them. They are exactly the sort of utterance which may well contain more than the conscious intention of the original teller. Sometimes, as we have already observed, knowledge of ordinary customs and assumptions in the society which generated a particular parable throws light on its original point and enriches our grasp of what it is about. But so many human situations are perennial or accessible through the intuitive imagination that whatever the specialists say, the parables and proverbs go on speaking. And their power does not depend on any grounding in historical fact. To treat the prodigal son as a historical person (as I have sometimes seen done) is to be at the same naive level as those who write letters to characters in television dramas. Parables are fiction, but like novels they may be 'true to life' fiction and therefore true without specific factual reference. The historical factuality of any story is not the most important thing about it.

Allegorical interpretation has often been criticized for turning biblical history into a great spiritual parable and reducing its actuality. But that should not, I think, be our principal worry about it. Of course the actuality of certain major events, like the life, death and resurrection of Jesus, is fundamental, but even such events are as important for their meaning as for their happenedness. There is a real sense in which to treat the whole thing as God's parable is a profoundly helpful way in to that meaning. The real objection to allegory is that it so often becomes crass exegesis, a rather pedestrian technique for explaining the joke in the sense of getting spiritual meaning out of every jot and tittle and domesticating the text to acceptable theology and practice. Allegory also made it too easy for people to make the text mean what the interpreter wanted it to mean, to turn the Old Testament into a collection of Sybilline oracles or a treatise in Platonic philosophy written in cypher. It was reaction against that kind of thing which produced insistence on a historical reading of the Bible. Yet has the reaction not gone too far? The allegorical approach had within it one exceedingly important element: namely the unashamed search for a meaning for us, a search which began in imaginative insights of the greatest profundity even if it did rather quickly run into the sand. That kind of imaginative grasp is inherent in interpreting poetry and parable, and is the best clue for interpreting other stories, even the central confessional stories of the Exodus and of Jesus which clearly have a tighter relationship to history.

For they are not history straight – if ever there was such a thing! Modern history-writing subjects itself to intense critical judgment in order to avoid distortion and propaganda, and yet good history writing always involves subjective judgment, selectivity, interpretation, telling the story from a perspective. This the Bible unashamedly does. The stories are told because they provide identity, because they offer examples. When the Church Fathers preached, particularly from the fourth century on but also earlier, they used the conventional forms of public speaking taught as a major part of the educational curriculum. One convention was to illustrate points by recounting stories of heroes from the past or using characters from the great classical literature, Homer or the great playwrights. The Fathers replaced these tales with the tales of biblical heroes, steeping their sermons in the biblical narratives; for this Christian literature was 'foreign' and far less well-known than the pagan myths. Perhaps we are now reaching the same situation, and we need to rediscover the potential of biblical stories as sermon illustrations – with a bit of imagination we might lead people to ponder things they never knew or only met in Sunday school years ago. The Bible is full of good stories, human stories of double-dealing, ambition, adultery – all the ingredients of the latest exciting television play! But how often we avoid these as unedifying instead of seeing them as a potential resource. We could do with listening to preachers from the black churches and learning from their 'narrative theology'. We do not know our Bibles well enough and instead we scrabble around for modern illustrations, most of which are far from memorable.

Interestingly enough, critical studies of the Old Testament, and increasingly of the New Testament, have emphasized that this was the context and purpose of the biblical story-telling in the first place. Re-telling the foundation-story of Israel, the tales of her great kings and prophets, was for the people the most legitimate form of theology. And the tales belonged to the people, to the community. There was no single inspired author taking it all down at dictation speed; those who wrote are largely anonymous, and what they wrote derived from the identity and consciousness of the community to which they belonged. Living in the Bible means for us a rediscovery of what it means to belong to that on-going community, to take its foundation stories as our foundation stories, giving us our identity, shaping our awareness, and pointing us to the future.

This means using the imagination. To use the imagination is not to retreat from fact into fantasy or from rationality into emotionalism. It may have inbuilt into it the danger of these things if we do not keep our critical faculties well exercised alongside our intuitive and constructive thinking, but in any serious thinking process both attitudes are involved. In the modern world there is a tendency to imagine that being rational or intellectual implies being logical, analytical, cold and critical and avoiding jumping to conclusions. But as we shall suggest in the final chapter, imaginative constructs and intuitive guesses are in fact the way progress is made, in science as much as any other field. It is this marriage between imaginative intuition and awareness of critical, analytical and historical questions which is essential for using the Bible as a theological resource. We dare not abandon critical and historical methods of studying the Bible, but we can learn again how to use them, how to train ourselves to know the Bible rather than knowing about the Bible, how to make these methods serve us in the work of interpretation rather than dictating to us. It is imagination that most of us need to recapture, though the dangers of subjectivist, nationalist and sectarian readings of the Bible today indicate that imagination cannot be allowed to run riot. The minister trained in critical study needs to share with the untrained in a new and creative dialogue, and then the Bible will become a genuine theological resource.

3
Using the Tradition as a Theological Resource

So far we have suggested that the very vocation of a minister implies theological seriousness, that the minister should be the theologian of the local church community. We have suggested that this should not invest a minister with dictatorial authority, but rather suggests that the ministerial role is educational in the best sense of being the 'midwife' of the church's theological reflection, understanding and celebration. In discussing use of the Bible this collaborative relationship between trained and untrained interpreters has been presented as the key to rediscovering the Bible so that it comes alive. The role of expert and non-expert must be affirmed, and their distinctive contributions re-integrated. The minister is the essential creative bridge-person.

The minister is also the specialist 'bearer of the tradition'. It is impossible for every church member to be in contact with the wider Christian community, whether we mean wider in the sense of spread throughout the world and in different denominational forms, or in the sense of being spread over many generations and many different historical cultures. The minister has had the opportunity to form wider contacts, within Methodism, on the ecumenical front, and with the past through study of church history. The minister mediates the wider tradition to the local group, which would otherwise be in danger of becoming ingrown, insular and even deviant. The minister needs to be plugged into the tradition and to be able to use it creatively to nurture fresh thinking about the meaning of the Christian faith today. He needs to understand past debates and discern how they remain important in the process of understanding the implications of

Christianity now. He needs to invite renewed debate about the central truths of the faith. But the importance of this is not generally recognized in the church. Let us again attempt to outline the current situation, and then reflect on why this aspect of the minister's role remains important.

A Seventh Day Adventist pastor was recently explaining to a group of university students how the issue of justification by faith was presently disturbing his church. I was immediately struck by the close parallels between the debates going on there about justification and sanctification, faith and works, and those that took place in John Wesley's lifetime. I was also struck by the seriousness of the debates. A hundred years or so ago, ordinary Methodist working people would attend lectures on such apparently abstruse topics as 'Entire Sanctification', regarding these matters as important. But today in Methodism, to put on such a theological lecture would be to invite an empty room, and to use such specialist theological language would be enough to make most people feel threatened or drowned in boredom.

And yet, the issues lurking behind such language are vital. They make a difference to how people live their lives. They raise questions about how scripture is to be understood and appreciated. Is the gospel about having faith or doing good? Does the gospel imply submission to certain prohibitions or freedom to do what one likes? Is the gospel a stimulus to loving action, but an optional extra, a kind of icing on the cake of natural human goodness? Or isn't it rather a profound critique of claims to human goodness and the offer of the transforming power of the Spirit to overcome sin? Now it may be that the traditional questions about justification and sanctification have their limitations: I suggest they over-individualize the message of St. Paul, distorting his emphasis upon a cosmic re-creation in Christ which involves far more than individual souls; but even so, the old debates did highlight important practical issues for the Christian believer. These issues are ignored at our peril. The theological controversies of the past are far from irrelevant.

Why then do they turn people off? Maybe we have to admit a certain lack of seriousness about the Christian commitment of many church people today. Certainly there is a good deal of uncertainty. But I suspect that that analysis is neither fair nor sufficiently fundamental. There is little social pressure on people to go to church these days, nor does it give anyone any worldly advantage. Attendance in itself implies some measure of seriousness about commitment. The reasons for lack of interest in past theological debates are to be found elsewhere. In the first place, our general cultural outlook has devalued the past; technological progress, social change and many other factors have separated us from our forebears in a way that has never happened before in human history, and made us look to the future, to the latest thing, rather than hoping to learn from what has gone before.

Secondly, our pluralist societies and the ecumenical spirit have tended to instil a general tolerance, and decent caring people are afraid of controversy, of rocking the boat. It is true too that theological debate has been deeply divisive in the past, and is so still where it is alive. The excommunication of deviants is a reality in the Seventh Day Adventist Church, and sadly the charismatic movement, partly because theological issues are alive again where its influence is felt, has often had a divisive effect in the churches. Fear of divisiveness is not by any means an insignificant factor, and if deeper theological discussion is seen to be desirable, it is essential we continue to live with diversity.

But finally, and this is a point requiring much wider discussion, people today tend to value immediate, practical experience over studying past thinkers and past controversies. Perhaps particularly in the church, though also elsewhere, experience in the sense of seeing for oneself has become a kind of shibboleth. In Methodism this is further encouraged by our own heritage: the internal evidence of the warmed heart, we have felt, is more effective than appeal to external evidences, arguments or proofs for the truth of Christianity. Today experience is usually taken to refer to what happens to us in day-to-day encounters, in direct confrontation or in emotional highs, and the fact is overlooked that experience includes our experience of thinking and of reading – confronting people removed from us by time or distance but present through the written word. Many of us have little opportunity to meet, say, real live Jews or Communists or even blacks in any more than a casual way. Indeed we often meet fellow-Christians of a different denomination or persuasion only occasionally. The chief way in which we can get to know in depth about people different from ourselves is by reading what they have to say, reading about their lives, their history, their beliefs.

Even those who do have personal contact find that their understanding is enhanced by reading material which provides further insight and a broader context and background. (Television is only a partial substitute, effective but extremely limited and selective.) How many tourists visiting a foreign country (other than just to lie on the beach) do without any form of guidebook? And is it not true that novels can often help us to discover what makes people tick, perhaps, most of all, novels that draw us into another culture? To leave out reading and study is to narrow our understanding of experience very seriously.

This general observation also applies more specifically. Too many of us have too individualistic a notion of the Christian faith and think our own private experience is all there is to it. Too many of those who have got beyond this, have too restricted an experience of the Christian faith, allowing only those with whom they share immediate fellowship to affect their own understanding. Of course things are changing: the ecumenical movement has not only made people aware of diversity, but has also made us more willing to share. But at the same time, even groups that transcend the traditional denominations have tended to acquire a certain homogeneous character, be they charismatic, evangelical or catholic. And local experience tends to be all: what we do and what they do we share, and perhaps we learn from one another. But just think – there are Christian groups dotted around the Arab world, cut off from the developments in western Europe for many centuries but with deep roots in the ancient tradition, which have a very different perception of what the Christian life is all about. Could it not be that we have something to learn from them too?

And to confine experience to the present also narrows it too much. Could it not be that we have a great deal to learn from past great periods of Christian thinking, practice and prayer, in spite of all the changes of which we are so conscious? Why should we suppose that because twentieth-century technology is superior, twentieth-century grasp of Christianity is also superior? To enter sympathetically into the thinking, and debating, preaching and praying of former generations is far from irrelevant. It may significantly deepen our own experience of these things. In fact it is to be alerted to diversity not only in the present, but also through the changes of history and the wide range of past cultures.

It is to have our tendency to define Christianity in our own terms challenged and to discern a community of saints that transcends our own time as well as place. It is to discover that things that puzzle us have often been issues in the past, even if expressed in different language and categories, and to realize that since people have been here before, their solutions are still worth looking at. It is to deepen our awareness of what it is all about, to claim our inheritance and enjoy its riches.

I suppose the best place for Methodists to begin to experience this is through engagement with the life and thinking of their founder, John Wesley. In any movement there is continuity, and much that we value as characteristically Methodist stems from our origins. So we might expect a natural chiming with John Wesley in spite of the time gap. If so we are likely to be surprised when actually faced with his writings, not least to discover features bearing upon the concerns of this chapter. 'How on earth did these dry rational discourses called his sermons convert uneducated working people?' will probably be the first question. They didn't, of course; the published sermons were for the doctrinal guidance of his assistants, and do not even treat the texts which according to the records he most frequently preached upon in the open. But the question which so immediately arises upon trying to read Wesley's writings, alerts us to the fact that to understand them we have to enter imaginatively into the eighteenth century world, a world in which reason was very highly prized, and claims to religious experience dismissed as 'enthusiasm'. Even our perception of standard elements in Methodist oral tradition, like the conversion-experience on 24 May 1738, is likely to be modified by an examination of the original accounts. So often we have heard how Wesley's heart was strangely warmed, how he felt he really did trust in Christ and Christ alone for salvation, and an assurance was given that he had taken away *his* sins, even his, and saved *him*, John Wesley, from the law of sin and death. The personal and experiential nature of this experience has always been emphasized. But it is not so often made clear that the effect of this was, first of all, to engage in passionate intercession for his enemies and persecutors, and secondly to doubt and question whether this really was the experience of faith since he felt no joy. This puts question marks against any tendency to think experience is sacrosanct and may not be questioned, or to think that experience is a purely personal matter. Further exploration of Wesley's writings soon reveals that he became acutely aware as the revival proceeded, of the dangers of identifying the experience of assurance with mere feelings. It was the fruits of the experience that ultimately mattered. Later he was to insist that faith could subsist with very little joy and that holiness and righteousness were as important as 'heart religion'. At the time it apparently freed him from concern about his own salvation so that he was able to pray for his enemies. Probably it was this release from self-concern which gave him the success in preaching which had previously eluded him; for it opened him to compassion and the ability to 'submit to be more vile'. The fruit of his conversion was that he no longer did charitable works simply because he ought to, but because he was liberated from the obligation of fear to assume freely the obligation of love. To describe conversion in terms of an emotional high or confine it to experience is to diminish it.

Another feature not often noted is that the occasion of this experience was not a highly charged evangelistic sermon, but a staid study group reading together, and what they were reading was Luther's *Preface to the Epistle to the Romans*, a classic of Reformation theology. Across two centuries, Luther opened the eyes and heart of John Wesley to the meaning of Paul's most difficult epistle, for him personally. It was not only John Wesley, but his brother Charles also who was led to conversion through Luther's words, this time by someone reading with him Luther's *Preface to the Epistle to the Galatians* as he lay on his sick-bed. Now these observations confirm that creative experience is not confined to immediate confrontation, but significant words transcend centuries and cultures through books, and contribute to personal experiences of significance.

In fact John Wesley's progress in understanding the Christian faith issued from the fruitful interplay of personal experience and wide reading. His contributions to theology were not original new insights but rediscoveries, criticism and assimilation leading to subtle combinations which integrated great truths enunciated by others, and dissolved poles of tension between them. Technically he was not a great scholar; his reading was somewhat haphazard and always exploited for practical ends. But he did appropriate the tradition, not as an optional outer dressing, but

Using the Tradition as a Theological Resource 39

as it were into his own bloodstream, so that experience and tradition were inseparable, two sides of the same coin. In fact we all do this to some extent, assimilating presuppositions from our environment quite unconsciously; but like Wesley, we may be further enriched by conscious and deliberate engagement with the tradition. So maybe we should explore his progress as illuminative for ourselves.

In 1725, stimulated by his father's suggestion that he should take holy orders, John Wesley began to take religious reading seriously. It was Jeremy Taylor's *Rule and Exercises of Holy Living and Dying*, Thomas a Kempis' *Imitation of Christ* and William Law's *Christian Perfection* and *Serious Call* which led him to dedicate all his life to God, all his thoughts, words and actions, seeking a religion of the heart and total devotion of body and soul. Some would go so far as to suggest that this was John Wesley's first conversion. Certainly it had immediate consequences: it issued in the Holy Club, nicknamed Methodist, a group of people who mutually set out to find and practice the way of perfect holiness. It also had long-term consequences: the search for holiness and righteousness, perfection in deed and word, remained even when later John Wesley recognized that self-justification or self-sanctification was impossible. Wesley criticized every one of these books, and later engaged in a fierce correspondence with Law; yet their influence was lasting and fuelled John Wesley's resistance to 'quietism' and antinomianism (see below). The range of John Wesley's reading is typified here. If Law was an older contemporary of the Wesleys, Taylor belonged to the previous century and a Kempis to the Middle Ages. Wesley soon embarked upon study of ancient Christian literature, and there is no doubt that the Fathers, especially those of the early monastic movement, influenced John Wesley's doctrine of Christian perfection. Some of the *Spiritual Homilies* attributed to Macarius, an Egyptian monk of the fourth century, were first translated into English by John Wesley and published in his Christian library. In his preface John Wesley brings out the significance and value of these homilies:

> Whatever he insists upon is essential, is durable, is necessary. What he continually labours to cultivate in himself and others is the real life of God in the heart and soul, that kingdom of God which consists in righteousness, and peace, and joy in the

Holy Ghost. He is ever quickening and stirring up his audience, endeavouring to kindle in them a steady zeal, an earnest desire, an inflamed ambition, to recover the Divine image we were made in; to be conformable to Christ our Head; to be daily sensible more and more of our living union with him as such; and discovering it as occasion requires, in all the genuine fruits of an holy life and conversation, in such a victorious faith as overcomes the world and working by love, is ever fulfilling the whole law of God. He seems indeed never to be easy, but either in the height and breadth or length of Divine love, or at least in the depths of humility.

For John Wesley, books both contemporary and from the distant past, provided great treasures. Admittedly he recognized the need for selectivity, for guidance in choosing what is profitable. Furthermore he was himself not a slavish but a critical reader. At the same time, he learned and developed by reading, while putting into practice and testing what he accepted from his study.

Clearly when he set out for Georgia as a missionary, John Wesley was more than a nominal Christian. But on that journey he met Christian people who had qualities he found he did not possess, notably a trust in God which transcended even fear of imminent shipwreck and death. Here personal contact stimulated a new search, largely pursued through his developing association with Moravian groups in Georgia, later in London and Germany. Yet John Wesley was not satisfied simply with experience and fellowship. He had to test everything he was told against scripture and tradition, and it was only as the new contacts threw well-known texts into better perspective that he was prepared to be convinced that faith was a gift he needed and had not yet received. It was because he found justification by faith in scripture and in the Anglican Reformation homilies that John Wesley began to search for and pray for faith for himself. Ultimately it was not those he knew personally who immediately stimulated the significant moment; rather it was, as already noted, the words of Luther. Yet it was the words of Luther read aloud in fellowship. The two things together, study in the context of communion with others, were the catalyst. Nor did John Wesley accept this new insight uncritically; once more he would attack what had influenced him most, precisely because it did not do justice to

Using the Tradition as a Theological Resource 41

that other aspect of the Christian tradition which had made such a powerful impression upon him. For totally devaluing works born of faith and love, he did not scruple to criticize Luther, or the Moravian leader Zinzendorff, later breaking with Moravian groups in London on precisely this issue. Against those who were so insistent upon the sole sufficiency of God's grace as to say that the moral law is abolished in Christ (antinomianism), John Wesley maintained on scriptural grounds the necessity of a life disciplined under God, methodical in its religious observances and directed towards avoiding evil and doing good. For him there was no justification by works, but works were the outcome of justification, the response of love to the love of God.

Thus it was that Wesley embraced the Reformation insistence on justification by faith while not forfeiting the endeavour to perform good works and aim at perfect holiness of life. In doing this he held together opposite poles that had more than once become unbalanced in the course of Christian history. Associated with this are other poles in tension which Wesley managed to hold together, God's sovereignty and human free will, original sin and Christian perfection, universal grace and conditional election. Indeed the evangelical revival posed precisely the theological questions we found unavoidable in the first chapter. Wesley's resolution of these tensions is not above criticism: there are theoretical difficulties in balancing original sin, prevenient grace and human responsibility, and difficulties both practical and spiritual in claiming that perfection is ever achieved in this life, all the more so in the light of Freud. Nor are the subtleties of his argumentation and the terminology produced by controversy immediately attractive to the modern reader. Yet wrestling with Wesley is worth the trouble. At the heart of his thinking are two sound and abiding principles: (1) we love because he first loved us; and (2) love implies practical action. These principles correspond with commonsense and have profound psychological force: unexpressed love cannot be called real love; and love is generated by love. It is more important to preach so as to win people's hearts for God and their neighbours than it is to prescribe moral solutions to the world's ills. Practical moral advice must be subsequent to the offer of the gospel of unmerited mercy, not substituted for it. Only thus can self-righteousness give way to the righteousness of Christ. John Wesley could look back on his pilgrimage and in mature reflection describe it as the movement from the faith of a servant to the faith of a son. The obligation of obedience remained, but the attitude of the heart was profoundly changed. Both states, he acknowledged, have value, but perfection belongs to those who love God with their whole heart, soul and strength, and their neighbours as themselves. That is his mature definition of perfection, a perfection not diminished by the fact of human defects like weakness, ignorance, misjudgments, failings and limitations; a perfection not confined to the ascetic and the monk, but potentially attainable by everyone in their everyday lives; a perfection which is not a static state but a dynamic process – and here Wesley must have learned from Greek theologians of the fourth century like Gregory of Nyssa.

Now all this brings us back to the very issues with which this chapter opened. For 'entire sanctification' is another way of speaking about scriptural holiness or Christian perfection. Such matters, I submit, remain relevant to our preaching and to our lives as Christians, and it is only by taking the trouble to explore our own tradition that the issues are properly focused and the right checks and balances maintained. Like Wesley we are likely to find that engagement with the tradition, carried out in an expectant and critical way, will stimulate a deeper awareness in ourselves. Study is an important element in an experience which comprises the whole of life and the whole of ourselves, our understanding as well as our actions and feelings.

But there are other ways too in which a study of Wesley can put into perspective the concerns voiced earlier. One issue raised was that bigotry and narrowness were the inevitable outcome of theological seriousness; maybe Wesley's acknowledged involvement in controversy has aroused such fears again. Wesley certainly lived in the midst of controversy and vigorously attacked many who had been his close associates. Particularly sharp was his disagreement with Whitefield over the doctrine of predestination – yet Whitefield had first led him into field preaching and open air evangelism. Besides, like Paul, Wesley found his mission aroused as much hostility as response, especially from those in ecclesiastical authority. Yet Wesley's ecumenism is beyond anything we would imagine humanly possible under the circumstances. He felt he had to distance himself from those he felt were misguided – some degree of conflict was inevitable. Here was no

Using the Tradition as a Theological Resource 43

bland liberal toleration. Yet at the same time he included in the perfection and holiness of the sanctified Christian a universal love, based on the command to love one's enemies, and spelt out in terms that included those with whom one did not see eye to eye doctrinally or devotionally. The catholic spirit was central, and included respecting and learning from a wide spectrum of styles of Christian profession. 'Think and let think' was his motto, but to interpret that as a lack of concern about doctrine and theology would be a gross misrepresentation of Wesley. Theological seriousness does run the risk of conflict, but conducted in the right spirit, conflict may be creative – indeed, it probably is an essential catalyst. To risk conflict is a harder and more disturbing road than settling for a woolly peace, but it is potentially more enriching. To prevent conflict becoming a damaging divisiveness is perhaps beyond merely human capacity, and probably in practice it eluded Wesley. To insist upon a renewed theological seriousness is to run risks, but risks that are worth taking as long as we hold fast to the catholic spirit.

Certainly, the catholic spirit of which we have spoken is nurtured by wide reading within and outside one's own tradition, the sectarian spirit by refusal to look beyond one's own group, or indeed by insistence on scripture only. For this, in many ways commendable, insistence fails to take account of the fact that scripture has to be interpreted, that interpretation requires a framework, classically given in the creeds, that interpretation necessitates making appropriate selection, that the appropriation of scripture requires its translation and adaptation into new languages, cultures and situations. All these things John Wesley knew. He claimed to be a man of one book (*homo unius libri*), and aimed systematically to forget everything he had read rather than collect secondhand opinions. He refused to accept anything that he did not find in scripture. He tested one scripture against another in order to uncover truth. He preached in the language of scripture. Yet, as we have seen, he forgot by assimilating, he received his framework of interpretation from the tradition of the church, from his catholic reading, and he was fully aware that interpretation involves not just reading scripture on one's own, but being aware of the knowledge and ideas of the contemporary world and relating the two – otherwise there would be no need to preach; just reading the Bible aloud would do. He thought his lay assistants should read for five hours a day, and read very widely, recommending the standard curriculum of classical literature used in eighteen century schools as well as early Christian Fathers like Ephraim Syrus and the writers of European pietism, not to mention his own publications. If they were not prepared to read they should give up preaching and return to their trade. He chided those who claimed to read only the Bible, accusing them of 'rank enthusiasm'. He was in fact an educator of his people, many of whom came from classes with no educational advantages. Pamphlet followed pamphlet, and from publishing he made a great deal of money, most of which he gave away. He made a new translation of the New Testament with notes for the ordinary English reader, and one of his most remarkable projects was the Christian Library. Over the course of seven years he selected and published a wide collection of Christian literature from many different periods and traditions, some items being translated into English for the first time. John Wesley recognized the difficulty for the average person of deciding what best to read in the course of a short life, and he wanted to give his people the height and depth of Christianity, through the medium of theological writings which agreed with scripture, and which were intelligible without being superficial. He therefore selected and abridged, tampering with texts in a way that would disturb the meticulous scholar but which served to highlight what he regarded as the essential matter. Perhaps this editorial programme provides us with a clue to the role of the minister. He needs to be, like John Wesley, the link in the chain between the world of the scholar and the ordinary church member. It is unrealistic to think that the average church-goer will wrestle with most of the theological literature available, whether we mean classic texts of the tradition or the burgeoning material produced by modern research and reflection. Ministers have had the advantage of learning a little of all this during training, and they are in the frontline of nurturing and assisting the exploration of the Christian tradition by their congregations. Undoubtedly they need continued help in their own selection of what is worth reading, and there is perhaps a job here for which better provision needs to be made, namely the fostering of ministers' continued study and engagement with the classic expositions of the faith, so that their own theological development never stops. But the urgency of this will not be apparent until it is more widely recognized that the minister has to act as mediator of the tradition: selecting, expounding and communicating it to the people.

If Wesley has any claim to be a significant theologian not just for Methodism but for all Christians, it lies in the extent to which he absorbed and integrated disparate elements, the theological traditions of the Reformation, the Middle Ages and the Patristic period, as well as contemporary writers, Catholic and Protestant. To absorb this and turn it into what has been called 'folk theology' for the mass of ordinary people was a remarkable achievement the like of which we could certainly do with now. I would suggest that the characteristic job of the minister largely lies here. As representative persons, ministers represent the collective body of the church in a number of ways, to the outside world, to God; but they also represent the wider church to the people, the local congregation. They are the bearers of the tradition, in a way that few ordinary members are. That is why the theological education of ministers is so important. Ministers are those whose responsibility it is to foster awareness of the heritage and a wider Christian perspective than the local congregation can have by itself.

4
Using Science as a Theological Resource

We live in a world which has been transformed by scientific enquiry and the technological applications of its results. One has only to compare the experience of the businessman in Venice in the fifteenth century with that of the merchant banker in London in the nineteen eighties to realize just how much their task has been revolutionized by science and technology. It is not simply that we now do things faster, or that there are opportunities which did not come to our forefathers, it is rather that our total view of what life is about has been dramatically changed by our understanding of the context in which it is lived. Our world is intelligible, potentially controllable, certainly adaptable to our concerns and interests; the scientist has ensured this by the careful and pervasive application of empirical and analytical techniques of enquiry.

Of course it is not necessarily all gain, there are questions which can and should be asked about the methods of science and perhaps more particularly about the way we apply the results of scientific enquiry. Nevertheless it is undeniable that we live in a world where not only the environment, but the very way in which we conceive of ourselves is largely conditioned by the fact of science and the consequent importance which is attached to its study.

And that in the minds of many ministers seems to bring the great divide. What has the minister to say in a world with which he is all too often unfamiliar? Few of us have a scientific background, few of us have the requisite mathematics, none of us has the time, to continue to be a scientist let alone to become one. And yet the issues which we face, for example those of pollution, of AIDS, of genetic engineering or information technology are undiscussable apart from some involvement with science. We have to come to terms with it, whether we like it or not. But in fact we should like it! The much neglected doctrine of creation, interpreted in the Christian tradition as it should be, by the notions of redemption, providence and grace, mean that there is gold in these hills if we can get at it. It is the minister's task to prospect and to mine, and to make something for us all of the raw material. It is not the task of the minister to be a scientist, but to be sensitively aware of scientific knowledge and to draw on it as a rich source for the celebration of human creativity.

We begin by pointing to truth, for we are all ultimately concerned with truth. At least if we are to be truly human that is what must fundamentally concern us. And in this endeavour theology and science are at one. But truth is not one-dimensional, it is many-faceted. Thus to begin to look at the human enterprise of scientific enquiry theologically is not simply a matter of applying truth as seen by the theologian to the truths as discerned by the scientist; it is the attempt to be open as a theologian to the truth about man that is presented by the fact that we can enquire scientifically, and that such enquiry has opened up to us with increasing security a knowledge of the world which is accurate, precise, and of unimaginable beauty and complexity. Of course the knowledge which we possess is not necessarily applied in a life-enhancing manner, neither is it always employed in the best interests of all mankind. But that is another story. The fact is that it can be translated into practical policies by us, and we can make judgments on whether they are good or bad. Furthermore it is also possible for us to contemplate policies with regard to the areas in which scientific research should be conducted. Thus it is not simply the consequences of science that should concern the theologian, but the fact that we can think scientifically; nor yet the fact that the applications of scientific knowledge raise questions about their value, but the fact that we can apply it at all. What sort of a world is it which permits us to understand it and to apply our understandings?

Theology is a form of enquiring which takes seriously the reality of God and the pertinence, indeed necessity for human maturity, of taking serious thought about him. It asserts that the world is a creation, not a mere universe, let alone the accidental, purposeless consequence of some set of random events. To claim that the world is a creation, in the Christian tradition, involves a belief in a creator who accepts responsibility for the world, and who has committed himself to making a success of what he has begun. But what he has begun is not something which he can achieve on his own. That is the paradox of the omnipotence of God as Christians conceive it to be. For what God wills in creating our world is the growth of persons through free and willing relationship with him and with one another in his world. It is a world which he loves and serves and to which he is committed; it is therefore also a world which we are called to love and to serve. Indeed it is the mutual love and service of the world by God and man in relationship through free commitment to one another that continually creates the world which God intends. But such love apart from understanding would be blind and ignorant, just as understanding and knowledge of the world or God apart from love will be barren and even destructive. But what sort of a God is it who makes a world which can be understood by us, and who relies on our loving co-operation for the fulfilment of his purposes?

Science has much to help us in tackling these questions and the minister has an enormous responsibility to get to grips with it and to interpret its significance. He is not looking for slick sermon illustrations which show that it is possible for scientists to be Christian believers, nor is she looking for coy references to intricate scientific knowledge in order to show how clever God is to have got things right. (After all the robin was not consulted about the breeding pattern of the cuckoo, and might not have appreciated the arrangement had it been put to her!) On the contrary, it is the minister's task to bring science, its methods and achievements, into the normal enquiring of all who are seeking God.

Since the majority of us have little or no science, or no longer read it if we had, this is not an easy matter. But in any study of the Bible and the tradition, it is important to bear in mind the influence which the contemporary understanding of the natural world had on the way in which ideas were shaped about God and his relationship to the world. One does not have to take suggestions of 'three-decker' universes literally, to recognize the fact that everyday experience and everyday expectations were indicative of ways in which God might be involved with his world.

We need therefore to be open now to the likelihood that what scientists are saying will involve patterns of discovery which question the ways in which we have been accustomed to think and talk about God. An obvious and depressingly current issue concerns the doctrine of creation. For it appears that there are still those who believe that faith in God requires literal adherence to statements regarding God's bringing the world into being as found in the book of Genesis. The truth is that we have new opportunities to make sense of these claims given the work of contemporary scientists, thus far from diminishing the context for religious reflection, it is enhanced.

But in order to grasp this opportunity we need to have a scientifically educated community; educated not only in the sense that it possesses some scientific knowledge, but that it recognizes the significance and limitations of scientific enquiry. Thus it is a sad feature of our situation that many children give up science at an early age, or may even have little science at all in their school. They thus lack a basis for a critical scientific understanding and judgment in a world increasingly shaped by science. The study of science in our curriculum has all too often been the prerogative of those who have special expertise or potential, whereas it is a normal necessity for each person. It is a natural thing to be curious about one's world and to want to structure one's experience in order to be able to take responsibility for it. Learning science is no more directed towards the provision of research scientists, than the learning of English is directed towards the creation of poets.

Now it is a delightful fact of human experience that we continually open up new areas of enquiry, and enrich our world by discovering new contexts for the creative application of familiar knowledge and techniques. An analogy here would be the creation of new languages or the elaboration of existing ones, the use of which draws our attention to things we had not noticed before, or relationships of which he had been hitherto ignorant. Natural languages do this themselves; German, Hindi, Swahili, Hebrew, for example, because of their different approaches to tense structure or their syntax show how it is possible to shape and respond to experience differently. What is most in mind here is, however, the language of the various disciplines of enquiry, biochemistry, nuclear physics, social anthropology, etc. Skill in

Using Science as a Theological Resource 51

any of these languages of enquiry on the part of any person, or increased facility on the part of the human race, enhances our response-ability, our ability to take account of our environment. This increased response-ability offers opportunities of responsibility too. The question is whether these aspects are kept appropriately in relation in the experience even of those who are given an education in science in the curriculum of schools, colleges and universities.

The memorizing of factual information, fed to one in an appropriate logical order is not what learning science is about, important as it is in its own context. Indeed even the memorizing of theories and the evidence for them is no substitute for discovering what it is to enquire scientifically. For this, we have to learn to observe, to relate, to calculate, to analyse the evidence and to make judgments about its likely truth or falsity with good reasons. We have to learn to be experimental, to be creative in our application of theories, to be adaptive in our approach to problems, to exercise delicate care in the way we associate apparently related experiences; and the crucial point is that these are as much as anything, qualities of the person. Scientific enquiry is, like every other form of enquiry, personal in the demands that it makes. This was always the case, but has become even more so, given the complexity of the operations in which we have now to engage, and the corporate nature of the work with which we are involved. Science is par excellence a team activity. Properly understood it involves the whole human race.

Thus to give the impression that scientific statements are true without question, even implicitly in the manner in which the teaching is done, is false to the nature of empirical enquiry which lies at the heart of it, and directs attention away from the fact that all scientific enquiry by human beings in relation. To imply that scientific theories are not in some way related to the social context and raise social questions is to be false to the basis and motivation for the enquiry which lies in human curiosity and the desire to enhance human happiness. To suggest that science is nothing more than a set of techniques and the acquisition of certain skills, is to ignore the point that the mere fact that knowledge has been and is gained by humankind by scientific enquiry, enlarges our vision of what it is to be a human being. It was Albert Einstein who remarked that 'The most incomprehensible thing about the

Universe is that it is comprehensible'. That is true. One might add that it is that very fact which necessarily involves the theologian; it is his conversation which sets things in the proper context where a true evaluation of what it is to be a human being might be made. A scientific education which has no room for questions and marvels of this kind, is not true to itself. What sort of a world is it which can be so understood? What can be said about human beings if they can so understand the world?

I mentioned above that the extension of scientific knowledge enhanced the capacity of human beings for response-ability, and that it potentially therefore extended the opportunity for responsibility. Furthermore, it was suggested, this responsibility is one which is in principle and in fact accepted by God. He deems us capable of, if not always willing to accept that responsibility. But in the same way as self-knowledge provides the necessary context of God's capacity and willingness to take responsibility for his creation, so human capacity for responsibility will only grow through self-knowledge. Thus science education cannot sensibly cut itself off from the rest of the ways in which human beings explore their various worlds; in an important sense all human activities are humanities, areas of human enquiring, and the distinction between science and humanities is from this point of view not simply misleading but dangerous. It is itself part of our confusing and prevalent anti-intellectualism. We are concerned in science education with the education of a person as a scientist, not with the programming of a computer, or the directing of a possible research worker. Any other view narrows the human perspective, and potentially stunts the maturity of the student.

The minister, through reading, through listening, through talking, preaching and writing, takes up into the question of God the experience which we as human beings are having as scientists. But that involves bringing to bear the significance of theological reflection on the process of scientific education. And if there are those who are excluded from this crucial area of experience, or who are given false hopes or assumptions through their experience of it, then it is our task by conversation, by analysis and enquiry to bring them into the fullest experience of human society, and to criticize the system which excluded them. It is a creative and necessary role; it is a theological role.

Since many people are interested in the question of the origin

Using Science as a Theological Resource 53

of the world, this would be a suitable starting point. There was a time when the theologian could safely regard this as an area in which he had special, not to say privileged, knowledge, but it is now the scientist who is the expert. Of course, it can be very misleading to say, 'Scientists now think that . . .', or 'Scientists tell us that . . .' After all, the authority of any such statements depends upon the reputation of the particular scientists who would agree that what is claimed is true, and the capacity of the speaker to be sensibly critical of the statement. Indeed such sentences are apt to imply an authority quite out of keeping with the feel of scientific enquiry itself. This would be true in the case of our understanding of everyday experience such as the nature of gravity or the swerve of a cricket ball; it is a *fortiori* true of questions about the origin of the universe. Yet the fact is that sensible and productive questions can now be asked scientifically about the origin of the world. The fact that this is so, is itself a matter of considerable theological importance. It is all the more important to observe this since these questions are not for the expert alone or the technical paper in a learned journal, they are of daily interest to those who see a newspaper reference carried about the space shuttle, and marvel at the probes which penetrate the atmospheres of Venus and Mars. The language of ordinary discussion already encompasses it. What are we doing as ministers to bring it into the orbit of theological reflection?

First, we might point out that the nature of the world is a matter of theological reflection already, since Christians claim that it takes its nature from the God who is its creator and who takes responsibility for it. But what does the fact that we can now talk scientifically about the way the world came into being mean for this long-standing theological enquiry? To me the astonishing and delightful thing is that we can talk at all about the origin of the universe in scientific terms. Here we are, human beings of finite intelligence and perception and limited education who, by diligent enquiry and imaginative experiments of great subtlety, can make proposals about the origin of the world which are stimulating and sensible. Who knows whether the present theories will withstand subsequent scrutiny? Whether they do or not, our creation of them is an important landmark in the development of our understanding of ourselves and our capacities. We have therefore to take account in our theologizing of a world which is increasingly found by us to be intelligible. Human powers of enquiry and reflection are such that the whole world is potentially open to us. This might imply that to the extent to which we take our belief in a creator God seriously, we shall have to entertain the question whether it is sensible to place him beyond our human understanding.

Secondly, there is the matter of time. We can assume that 4004 BC is no longer a contender for the date on which the world began. Yet it is likely that the world began finitely at some huge distance of astronomical time. It is a conjecture what that date might be. What is intriguing is our capacity to cope with the absolutely vast tracts of space and time which are implied by the theories we now find so illuminating. To list some facts and figures is to refer to common knowledge on the part of an increasing proportion of the population – a matter which is itself significant. For example, the 'big bang' which occurred at the beginning of the universe was some 15,000 million years ago, and our solar system came into being 10,000 million years later. The Milky Way galaxy, of which the earth is a part, is made up of some 100,000 million stars of which no more than 3,000 can be seen by the naked eye in the very best conditions. These stars are arranged in a disc about 100,000 light years across, and 2,000 light years thick. The huge increase in our knowledge of the universe as a whole has come about almost exclusively from the analysis of electro-magnetic radiation (i.e. light, radio waves, X-rays, etc.) which travel at the speed of 3×10^{10}cm per second. Since therefore the information we record on photographic plates has often taken millions or thousands of millions of light years to reach us, the further away the object we are studying, the earlier we reach into the past of the universe.

There was a time when such dimensions would have dwarfed or even depressed any sense of our own worth, but we now take satisfaction from being in some sense capable of managing them. Far from indicating that the world is beyond our control, it suggests that we are beginning to inhabit the whole universe, from start to finish, intellectually, emotionally and imaginatively. It is as if we have really begun to get the measure of things spatially and temporally; as though we have our hands round it all.

We have been taught to make the fundamental distinction between how and why, and led to accept the view that whereas

Using Science as a Theological Resource   55

theology is concerned with the whys, science is concerned with the hows. Whatever truth there is in this, and there is some, the distinction must always be blurred for the theologian. The 'how' of things, must have implications for the 'why'. And the fact is that from the scientific point of view, the world is a place where we increasingly feel at home. We need to take that into account when we reflect on God's relationship to the world and to us.

Thirdly, there is a feature of the origin of the world which has fascinated some scientists. Circumstances would only need to have been different in a very small degree from the beginning for the world to have been incapable of sustaining human life. Furthermore, the regularity which is implicit in the origin would only have to vary slightly over time for us to be denied the opportunity to understand the world with the certainty and optimism that we in fact have. It is as if the world was made with man in mind. What has been called 'the anthropic principle' was first discussed by Carr and Rees in *Nature* in 1979, but theologians need to be wary of making too much of it. It is an interesting proposal, but no more; it certainly constitutes no proof of God, or even another argument. What it does is show how science and the whole enterprise of scientific enquiry can be humanized; and that is a matter of some importance.

Contemplation of, and reflection on the origin of the universe is involved with matters which are beyond our control; the nature of human life and, in particular, human genetic engineering, is not necessarily so. We want to know why the universe is as it is and so we are eager to enquire about the origin of the world. But we also want to know why human beings are as they are, and whether we can do anything to change this. There may even be a glimmer of a connection between the two, since physical and chemical processes are themselves part of the evolutionary pattern.

Progress has been notably rapid in genetics. Indeed the speed of the developments has been such that there is some public disquiet about it. Is it sensible that we should be able to carry out experiments on live foetuses? What are the moral issues raised by the availability of techniques for recombinant DNA? Are we entering a period of history when it will be possible to design our human society by genetic engineering? Even if it was possible to breed a supremely healthy and intelligent race, would we be justified in doing so? I only raise these questions because, with this topic, there may be an immediate sense that at last we have moved into an area where theological reflection is relevant. After all, if the minister has nothing to say about values and morals, what has he got left to talk about? The answer to this is God; and if the minister is not talking about God, celebrating his presence, and directing attention to him, then he is wasting his time. So, does the fact that we are learning more about genetics, and gaining increasing techniques to exploit this knowledge, in crop husbandry, the treatment of congenital disease, and the control of the population, have anything to say to us about God and his responsibility with us for the fulfilment of his purposes in creating the world?

The first thing to say is that God must believe that we are in principle capable of using such knowledge responsibly, or he would not have given it to us. There is a great deal in the biblical tradition about the responsible use of knowledge, but nothing whatever to suggest that humans should seek to be ignorant. The parable of the talents can be applied to the human race as a whole and not simply to individuals, so if we have collectively and in community the ability to explore, for example, our own genetic structure, we should do so. Indeed, had we been intended not to do so, presumably we should not have been endowed with the intelligence and imagination to even aspire to it. Of course we could come to the conclusion that a particular area of knowledge should not be made use of. Would we, for example, wish to breed selectively for uncritical obedience, even if such a possibility were to materialize? But the crucially exciting aspect of this matter is that God has so much trust in us as human beings that he supports us in the acquisition of knowledge and is able to manage himself in relation to us whatever the use to which we put it. In other words, he is not subject to the debilitating despair which we often feel when things go wrong. He is serious in his commitment to the purposes he has in creation, which purposes require our willing co-operation. He neither enforces obedience, nor destroys us when things go wrong. He will use our exploring and its applications in his creating.

Secondly, this line of argument offers us a new insight into the nature of God's omnipotence. Given the vastness of the universe as a whole, and the infinite complexity of the arrangements in

Using Science as a Theological Resource 57

relation to genetics, it is too easy to romanticize the power of God. 'Just think how enormously powerful he must be to have done all that!' And, of course, one could add how clever he must have been to have thought it up, and how affectionate he must have been to want to do it at all. This is not the point to which we should deflect attention, however, if we want to understand the traditional attributes of God. These terms are reflexive in the first instance; they do not refer (except by implication) to the way God relates to his world. God had to know himself thoroughly, if he was to be capable of acting freely in relation to whatever was not himself. If he had not known himself thoroughly, he might have been put into a position by his own relationship with creation, where he discovered an aspect of himself which he could not control, and which therefore diverted his ability to give himself wholly to his creation. When coping with himself, he would not be free to love his world. But Christians claim that since God knows himself thoroughly, and is therefore utterly in control of himself, he can in every way and in every context freely love the world which he has made. As we traditionally say, God is omniscient, omnipotent, and therefore all-loving. This understanding of God is precisely witnessed to by our acquisition of knowledge. We are capable of acquiring it because we are so endowed by God himself. God is not willing therefore to prevent us from acquiring whatsoever knowledge we choose. Furthermore, even when we misuse the gift of knowledge, God does not interfere (even if he could, and I'm not at all sure that he could) to prevent us. On the contrary, he is capable of continuing to work with us in love, because he knows that in fact we are capable of making use of our knowledge sensibly and responsibly if we so choose. Such faith on the part of God enlivens our own faith, and offers new hope.

But of course it gives a particular perspective to the acquisition of scientific knowledge, and a special insight into the responsibility which it brings which has implications for scientific education to which I have already alluded.

It is also important to note that scientific knowledge is often not used responsibly or with understanding and that when this happens there are consequences. The landslip at Aberfan came from the dumping of slag onto ground which was riddled with underground springs. The implications of this were not understood. Nuclear energy may be used to enhance human life or to destroy it; the risks involved in using some new drugs turn out to be unacceptable. It is not only possible to apply scientific knowledge carelessly with disastrous consequences, it is also possible that present knowledge makes it unreasonable to carry out certain experiments which would otherwise be desirable. But, of course, the desire to know may override sensible caution. For example, it would be reasonable to regard the proposals for the generation of electricity by the Severn barrage as requiring the actual construction of the system, since no limited experiment could predict the consequences to wildlife, water level, and ecological balance accurately. To experiment without due attention to the risks, or to apply knowledge without care is to invite the wrath of God, through hubris. It is not that God punishes, or acts inconsiderately without regard for human care; it is the simple consequence of the rational and affectionate purpose of an intelligent being who invites rational and considerate behaviour on the part of human beings, his partners in creation.

But what is science anyway? There are many reasons why we do not tackle the fact of science or the implications of scientific enquiry in our theological reflection. The most obvious is that we know little science, and are anxious not to look foolish in the presence of those who do. Another is the altogether misleading authority which science and its technical applications still seem to have in our society. A third might be that too many of us do not believe that there are any stimuli for theological reflection which flow from the results of the work of scientists. Yet another concerns the desperate theological illiteracy from which we suffer, which means that we all too frequently lack the resources to grasp at difficult questions for ourselves, let alone move into worlds where we know that in order to learn we shall have to admit and expose our own ignorance. We might help ourselves, as well as help others, if we note three features of science. First, the application of the techniques of science leads to the acquisition of genuine knowledge. We have so far avoided terms like objective and subjective, their use can be so misleading; yet the fact is that science provides us with objective knowledge, in the sense that it can at least be publicly tested. To test something publicly and to agree with all other interested and qualified parties is not necessarily to show that the scientific description corresponds

Using Science as a Theological Resource 59

with how things actually are. After all there may be collusion between those involved, whether it be intentional or simply the condition which human enquirers find themselves in. Nevertheless the area of real doubt reduces as the number and generality of successful predictions increases until eventually the doubt which remains can be called only a philosophical doubt. Logically it would still be true to say that science did not therefore deal with certainties in particular cases; what would be unreasonable and silly would be to suggest that science was not a set of ways by which genuine knowledge was acquired by human beings. It is important to say this since there is a present tendency to claim that since science is the work of human beings and does not deal with certainties, the knowledge offered by this means is insignificant when put in the context of theological enquiry. On the contrary, no theological discussion will be significant which ignores how we now customarily think about the world in which we live, and ourselves in relation to it. To ignore scientific knowledge would be to disqualify any claim to knowledge which theological enquiry might itself wish to make.

Secondly, even if science is not simply the result of human imaginative effort, but is rigorously disciplined so as to take account of the physical experience we have of the world in order to bring knowledge of it, it certainly is a human activity which employs the imagination on observations and data, and not only the intellectual powers of disciplined analysis. Thus we can rule out the thought that science simply describes what is there, as if the techniques of enquiry uncovered exactly what was going on. The task of scientific enquiry is much more imaginative than that. For example, in asking some questions one precludes the possibility of getting answers to others, so that seeing things whole is always and necessarily a matter of judgment, and the exercise of the imagination in holding together the apparently incompatible. This is not particularly a problem, though non-scientists often seem to think that it ought to be. However, whether electricity is best explained by wave-mechanics or by particle-theory, depends at least as much on which mathematics fits the problem with which one is dealing, as on whether we can decide in fact which is really true. How much better to have a couple of pictures or models with which to operate, rather than one. The taste and judgment of the scientist is therefore often paramount in selecting the appropriate theory, and notions of beauty and simplicity will not be irrelevant.

Thirdly, it is a restless activity which is never satisfied with the pictures it draws, or with the consequences of the application of the knowledge it provides. And since it is not fixed, it is something for which human beings can take responsibility. Thus not only does science, by its own extension of human response-ability extend the potential opportunity for human responsible action by the fact of its own existence at all, it raises questions about the nature and extent of human responsibility, per se. Questions can legitimately be asked about the areas into which human beings should enquire, both in principle, and in respect of the available resources or the purposes for which the enquiry is required. The extent to which it is possible to set limits in any of these contexts depends upon political, social and economic circumstances. These contexts are much to the fore in present discussion. Thus the government is increasingly taking steps to direct scientific research in our institutions of higher education in order to ensure that it serves the economic well-being of British industry; and industry criticizes the way in which society in its value systems demeans and does not encourage entrepreneurial activity or the practical implications of scientific enquiry through technology. But these are not the only relevant contexts.

The further crucial context is that of belief. What do we believe it is that human beings are called upon to take responsibility for? The Christian tradition argues that God has called humanity to take responsibility with him for the whole world and the way it is, and for all people and the enjoyment they have in this life. This is a tall order, but it certainly places responsibility in both a global (not to say universal) and personal context. As a result of some of what we now know, we can begin to glimpse the sense and extent of this claim. For example, if the phenomenon of acid rain is as serious to the natural environment as many believe it to be, then we can take thought as to the means of preventing it. Or if we calculate that the world cannot provide with known resources for the energy demand of the twenty-first century, we take (as we are) steps to ensure that new resources will be available. And even, though it is only just possible, if we thought that a particular area of research, such as toxic gases for military purposes was too dangerous for us to explore since security could

Using Science as a Theological Resource 61

never guarantee that it would not fall into the wrong hands, we could decide not to take matters further. The belief that we have regarding the nature of humanity's work in the world in association with God means that these questions have a qualitative and factual relevance to what we choose to put our resources into. And so one might say that scientific enquiry is one of the most fascinating ways in which we equip ourselves as a human race, to take responsibility with God for the nature and condition of the world in which we live. Indeed it is a means whereby we make possible our share in the creative activity of God the Father, and make a reality of the redemptive work of Jesus the Christ, and joy in the delightful presence of the Holy Spirit who sustains us. The work of the scientists ennobles our vision of ourselves, our sense of humility in the presence of the God whose self-giving is the condition of our humanity.

At any rate it is worth a great deal more thought than we customarily give it.

5
Using History as a Theological Resource

There has been a huge ferment on social and political matters in the church. There are no easier topics on which to stir up controversy than the role of women in society, or racism, or the role of the church in politics, to take but three examples. The amount of literature available on social and political issues from a Christian point of view is enormous. Now it is clear that theological concern is for human well-being and that this must include every aspect of what it is to be human. We rightly, therefore, include physical health, educational opportunity, political freedom, economic potential and community identity in this; only making a mistake when we think that this involves some new decision or re-orientation on the part of the theological task. There always have been times, as any study of history will attest, when Christians have glimpsed and celebrated the wholeness of humanity in their service of human needs. The study of history has some point if it draws attention only to this and prevents us from the distorted impression that our generation has at last reached the high ground of truth on this matter. Of course, we may have to learn the truth all over again, but in that the study of history will not simply be helpful, it will be necessary.

We are therefore concerned in this chapter with the importance of history, with historical enquiry, and the significance for the minister of being at least aware of its results, even if there is no time to be a student of history. Of course the study of history may amount to no more than antiquariansim – that is, the discovery of what went on in the past, or what the original purpose was of the remains of buildings or the objects which we find around us now. While this may be interesting for its own sake, and should not be dismissed as completely irrelevant, the student of history is concerned with much more than this. The historian is curious about the context and process of past circumstances and environment which result in a world of the kind we now have, and possible futures of the kind we contemplate. At one time in our attention to history we were apparently concerned with no more than the external political realities, as if these were the only things that mattered. Thus there were written the biographies of great men, and accounts of the broad sweep of political intrigue and military prowess; there was even sought some common thread running through it all which might account for the success and failure of cultures. Now nothing escapes our interest as we perceive with growing clarity the diverse nature of the influences, ideas, patterns of social structure, economic experience, art and philosophy, hopes and illusions which contribute to the world we are. And all and any of these (and many more), can be focused upon the history of a nation state, the European situation, the future of architecture, the role of religious belief, the conflict between East and West, the pattern of population distribution, and so on.

Such enquiries are not incidental pastimes for those who have the leisure to take account of them. On the contrary their study is the necessary condition of any judgment about change or continuity that might be made by a political party, an industrial company, in educational provision, or in town planning. Indeed without an historical sense, which can only be acquired by diligent attention to history, and to the results of historical enquiry, the human race will simply be ploughing around in a bog without sense of direction or knowledge of its position. Irish affairs are surrounded by the miasma of illusion and myth which makes nonsense of the possibility of present political progress or responsible action. Nowhere could it be more obvious that there is a need for genuine historical enquiry to make possible an objectivity, a humility before the enormity of some of the facts, and a new commitment to build a future. Historical experience is a real influence in the conduct of affairs and in the judgments which we make, to ignore it is to be mastered by it. We may only need a limited number of experts who act as our scholars in historical research, though it would be interesting to speculate on the means whereby one could ascertain precisely how many that should be

Using History as a Theological Resource 65

for the health of the community. But in any case we assuredly need the vast majority of the population to be familiar with historical categories, capable of assessing an historical argument, and engaging in the discussion of issues with historical sense.

The Christian religion would be false to its roots and lose its identity if it even suggested that history could be ignored. Its holy book, the Bible, takes history with the utmost seriousness. Such a statement should be made with caution, since there are apparently still those who could take it to mean that the Bible is an historical statement of God's dealings with his people, most especially in the biographies of the life of the saviour Jesus Christ found in the gospels; any such claim would of course be false. The Bible is not an historical textbook, neither are there any biographical accounts of the life of Jesus whom we call the Christ. In fact the attention which the Bible gives to history is much more significant and more revealing than this. Since human beings have been placed in a world for which we have some responsibility, that must imply a responsibility in some sense for history – both for what happens and what has happened as well as what will happen. The events which involve human beings are not accidents, nor are they events which happen apart from the free choices which human beings make either individually or collectively. Furthermore, since we are involved in a linear view of historical processes and not a cyclical view, we therefore have some opportunity to take responsibility for the future; it need not be like the past. Indeed this is the most challenging insight to be gained from an understanding of the doctrine of the resurrection – the future, whether personal or that of society, does not need to be like the past. It is, of course, related to it and is not discontinuous, therefore the resurrection is of a recognizable kind and continuous with past experience from which it learns and which it embraces. So in the Old Testament there are several attempts to come to grips with the past, in order to see in what way the writers could shape the questions regarding present decisions. The Books of Kings (or its material) were rewritten and re-interpreted by the writers of the Chronicles in order to see if there was another way in which sense might be made of their historical experience and a different future opened up. The New Testament constantly celebrates and points to the new past as well as the new future, both of which are necessary if there is to be any reality in the present freedom to which the gospel so thankfully points.

So what can we learn from the study of the past? This can be a very simplistic and misleading question. History does not teach us lessons, neither is the purpose of the study of history to improve the moral basis of our choices in the present. However, we learn from history insofar as we place ourselves with delicate judgment in a position to get the hang of what is going on, and use that experience to inform our choice of what it is worthwhile putting our minds and hearts to now. And it has all to be done with the fullest possible awareness of the fact that not everything is under our control, that we do not and never could aspire to direct the future. What we can do, however, is to grasp the truth as we discern it, and experiment responsibly with it.

There is a form of essay writing on historical matters which, it seems, is willing to list the eleven reasons for the First World War. But we all know that life is more complicated than this. In the case of history the situation is made most difficult by the fact that we are dealing each time with individual and special circumstances. Only recently have we in the West been capable of recognizing the significance of this remark when trying to understand the Eastern European bloc. Because each country (Romania, Czechoslovakia, Poland, the German Democratic Republic, not to mention the very particular cases of Albania and Jugoslavia) has a distinctive and valued historical experience, the way in which each relates itself to Marxist theory, and the way in which each Communist Party functions to manage its relationship with the whole population is different in every case. Indeed, paradoxical as it may seem to our western notions of what constitutes freedom, there is a sense in which it is Marxism's very assumption of commonality which has emphasized and revivified the national, and in some cases religious, traditions of the state. Each case is different; each situation has a particular explanation. Each case requires the close attention of personal scholarship and the comparison of the work of many minds, if we are even to begin confidently to get the hang of it.

When applied to history, cause and effect are slippery concepts. They seem to imply a security which they cannot offer when employed in historical analysis. Nevertheless they are important. And some answers can be given to some questions. We could

Using History as a Theological Resource 67

take the analogy of a rugby match. Our team may have lost and consequently it will be important to come to terms with this fact and to take steps to rectify the situation in future seasons if not next week. So why was it? The other team had larger forwards. But they were not as fast as ours. They had a better spirit amongst the team. But would that have been effective if they hadn't scored an opportunist try in the very first minute? They had an all-round team, whereas we quite clearly had some weak performances on the day. But we had the outstanding player. The referee was not willing to be advised by our supporters, notwithstanding the fact that they gave him the benefit of their wisdom freely and often. But the match was at home, and we should have been encouraged by their support. Our captain had had a quarrel with his wife, whereas the opposition captain was celebrating the birth of his first child. They came from a town which is down on its luck and they believe that it is up to the team to win matches and give the people something to shout about. It was in the stars, and their astrologer told them they were destined to win. How many more reasons could be given? And in any case what exactly is the relationship between the presentation of such reasons and the actual causes which led to the game being lost? Certainly we could not in any circumstances put together these reasons in a series and draw the logically necessary conclusion that our team was bound to lose. There would be nothing incompatible, nothing which could therefore be said to be necessarily untrue to history in offering all these reasons why our team should or even would lose, and then discovering that we routed the opposition.

The same is, of course, true in historical analysis. We explore the reasons for the failure of the Treaty of Versailles in 1919, and may be persuaded by the fact that the terms themselves made a further outbreak of hostilities more likely. The Armistice enabled the German armies to return home in good order and the politicians to claim that they had not really been defeated – indeed, that they had been betrayed. The economic clauses of the treaty were unenforceable, because no state could pay full indemnity for the cost of such horrendous conflict, while at the same time the attempt to enforce them stimulated an ignorant self-righteousness on the part of some of the allies, and a rancorous resentment among many sections of the German population. Ignorance of economic realities and political ineptitude combined to make the provisions of the Treaty of Versailles significant in the way that we now regard them. But this distinction is important. We may rightly regard the treaty as a cause of the Second World War, but it did not make war inevitable; it involved also the combination of that treaty with the consequent indecisive or timid policies of the USA, France and Great Britain, which allowed Germany to re-arm, and a notable megalomaniac to persuade millions that he could lead them to a brave new world. The point is that decisions made in resolving conflicts, whether international or national, military or economic, social or political, have to be managed in their effects. It is simply not the case that in history causes have inevitable effects. It once more makes sense to talk of the role of the human in history, our capacity to take responsibility, and to shape, not only what the future might be, but what the past means, by the choices we make today. But we do have to be working at the question of what the past is about if we are to take part in the process.

What are you doing? is not such an easy question to answer as might appear at first sight. Suppose that you are found by a friend in the act of cementing two stones together and you are questioned about it, the following dialogue might reasonably take place:

> What are you doing?
> I'm holding some stones.
> Really!
> I'm cementing two stones together.
> Sure.
> I'm arranging these stones with others.
> H'm?
> Perhaps you could say I was building a wall.
> Go on!
> I'm working with others to build something important.
> Ah, now we are getting somewhere – so you are not just taking exercise!
> I'm actually building a cathedral to the glory of God.
> So that's it. In that case I can tell you that what you are really doing is providing the means whereby yet more generations of human beings will be enslaved, and further delaying the revolution which will save mankind.
> On the contrary, I'm sharing the creation of an environment

Using History as a Theological Resource 69

where men and women can begin to feel the reality of God's presence, and by sharing in that celebration, gain courage to accept the freedom they already have. From that will come the revolution in our relationships which we all really long for.

If there is a need for such a dialogue to come to an end? How would we decide which of the two views was right? And what relevance do the beliefs of those who act in the situation have on the meaning of what is happening?

Let's take these questions in turn. And let us apply them to the matter of historical analysis. Thus, first, is there any reason why discussion of what is going on should ever come to an end? It will only happen when it has ceased to be interesting to discuss the case, and even that could be a very temporary matter; and it could be a contingent matter depending entirely upon the lack of an inspired and imaginative writer on the topic. For example, Henry VIII has continued to excite the interest of the ordinary person for all sorts of reasons, including his forays into Europe, the English nationalism and independence from the Pope, the exciting religious ideas which took over the country, the development of a more rigorous system of administration, and not least, his concern for the dynasty and the number of his wives. And to this must be added the quality of the historians who have been attracted to study his reign. But what was going on really?

It is the little word 'really' which seems to attract us, and yet which is in fact so unsettling, as if despite all these things which were happening, they were simply signs or tokens of what was going on behind the scenes. Now it is always sensible to recognize that there are forces and influences which could be taken into account, but which we have not become aware of since we have not the tools to deal with them. But it is unreasonable to be preoccupied by them. The fact is that Henry VIII did play with the notion of conquest in France and when that did not work, sought to establish himself as the peacemaker of Europe with the help of Wolsey. It is also true that in order to preserve the house of Tudor against the threat of dissolution through lack of an heir, Henry sought to divorce Catherine of Aragon which brought him into conflict with the Pope, and with Charles V, the Holy Roman Emperor. This meant that a king who had so recently written in defence of the Catholic faith became head of a church which was national though not Lutheran. Indeed the extent to which the confusion of political and religious ideas took years to resolve can be found in the results of the increasingly sensitive work of local historians who show the tardiness with which reformed ideas spread amongst an often uninterested or unwilling population. This is not unnatural when one reflects that central government would be interested above all in continuity and security and new religious ideas would be untested in this regard and could even be shown to be suspect. How natural, therefore, that sound administration, above all sound financial administration and local administration, should be a priority. Far from the reign seeing a triumph of local democracy with the election and support of local MPs in Parliament, Henry became increasingly suspicious of a body which might not do his will, and which might even withhold the money which was necessary for foreign security. Central direction was the order of the day. So when should the debate come to an end? When will we be able to say, 'Oh, I see, so that's what it is about'. Never, of course, because each generation, each historian excited by the period, each school of historical enquiry, each method of historical analysis, will want to have a look at this crucial period in English and European history, and offer its view of what was going on. And most, if not all, will be valuable, though some will clearly add more to our understanding than others.

Secondly, how would we decide which of two views was right? In strict terms, this might be a naive thing to try and do. But on the other hand, if the choice is between a view which suggests that the French Revolution was the consequence of a series of catastrophic harvests, and the view that the condition of working people in town and country had nothing to do with the situation, then one could argue that the same evidence would count both in favour of one view and against the other. Thus, if there were conspicuously good harvests in the years from 1775–1789, the first theory would be undermined and the second at least given some support. But given that any number of views might have some truth in them, and that no historian of repute would be prepared to declare unilaterally for any one account, the question is always a matter of judgment. Thus what was happening at the French Revolution will be a matter of judgment, but it was and always will be a complex matter. For example, when one looks in

Using History as a Theological Resource 71

the province of France away from the many urban centres, one may find a conflict of issues. After all, at a time when news travelled relatively slowly in a society which was inevitably conservative in its nature, it would not be surprising if groups of people supported the revolution (who said it was a revolution, anyway?) for reasons which they then found were not part of it at all.

And, thirdly, what bearing does the intention of the agent or agents have on the nature of the events? Just supposing it is known what the intentions were which the agent or agents believed he or they had, then they will only be one of the influences which contributed to what was going on. But the intentions are interesting and relevant pieces of information since they do plausibly indicate the sorts of things which people with influence, or who would like influence, at a given time felt that it was worth trying to achieve. They also constitute an area of suspicion and criticism which is exploited in contemporary political debate. For example, in the Green Paper on 'The Future of the Welfare State', it is assumed that we cannot afford to continue a system which has, on other grounds, failed to fulfil its promise. In order therefore that a larger number of those really in need may be given greater support, it is necessary for the wider community to become more self-reliant. Private schemes of education, and private provision of an increased share of the costs of housing, medical service and insurance need to be encouraged in order to lighten the burden on taxation. But is this the real intention of the government? Is it not rather that, having determined to precipitate a leaner and fitter economy, and therefore brought about the largest increase in unemployment in order to keep the unions under control, there simply is not enough money in the tax system to pay for the unemployment benefit, and all the other commitments? The latter have therefore to be cut. What is really going on? Intentions are certainly relevant and to be taken into account, because they make a difference to the way in which one assesses the situation. Of course, whatever the intention, one may still judge that the policy is mistaken and needs to be resisted.

This recent example illustrates the fact that the historian, as also the participant in the discussion of contemporary policy and its consequences, is himself involved with what he or she is enquiring into. There is not and there should not be an unbiased historian any more than there should be an unbiased politician. In describing and giving an account of what (it is believed) is going on, imagination, judgment, tact, style, experience and common sense will all influence and give one's interpretation a nudge. History is, after all, human history; and the historian helps us to keep our responsibility for it alive.

There is a hideous confidence in some theologies which is not simply dangerous, but which is actually the very antithesis of the Christian position. For example, there are some fundamentalist evangelicals, who seem to believe that the world is heading for Armageddon and that, therefore, a nuclear conflict should not necessarily be resisted. After all God will see to it that sufficient of the righteous in the capitalist West will survive to make a go of it in the brave new world of faith which will ensue. Such confidence in an inevitable future is used to justify behaviour which tends to bring it to pass; understanding the countries of the Eastern bloc, attempting to work with them whenever possible, reawakening historical enquiry which may give insight into possible alternative futures is reckoned to be pointless, and indeed contrary to the will of God. The root of such beliefs is fear not sense, and certainly not faith. It is obviously inconsistent with the nature of historical enquiry as it has been discussed here, and must be resisted. The future and the past are both aspects of the present for which we are responsible. To close down the future as if there were no alternative is not a view open to the Christian.

To claim to know the future in this way is to claim to know more than God knows himself. A child is a human being without the riches of experience who does not yet therefore know who he or she is. As a totally available space, he or she is determined by every influence and every gift that is offered; only in the light of experience does the shaping and testing come which enables us to become ourselves. On the other hand, to want to know the future, or even to believe that the future can be fully known is to give in to the illusion that by our own choices we can determine what it will be. Our desire to do this stems from a continuing ignorance of ourselves, and a fear that the future is bound to bring problems with which we cannot cope, or people with whom we cannot co-operate; we must therefore determine what will happen. But God is neither the child, nor the aggressive individualist, whose confidence and bravura stem from fear and self-

Using History as a Theological Resource 73

delusion. He is above all whole, and possesses full knowledge of himself. What need has he therefore to know the future? On the contrary, as the one who is the creator, and whose purpose is to make a world of persons he is precluded from determining the future apart from the co-operation of the world of persons with which he is working. What he knows is that no matter what occurs, or what choices are made, he can and will be able to work with it to fulfil the purpose of his creating.

It is this insight which lies behind the attribution of eternity to God, which places time itself in the context of God's relationship to the world, and which should illuminate our perception of what it means to refer to God as gracious and all-loving. It is not that nothing makes any difference to him because he is atemporal, and therefore occupies no space, has no body and therefore feels no pain. Rather, that no betrayal or misunderstanding of his purpose on the part of man, takes the world outside the capacity of God to go on working to bring it into the fullest possible relationship with him. His eternal presence is an eternal present which means that the past and the future are both alike a matter of creative choice. The future is in our hands.

Of course this does not mean that the past can be ignored, or that it disappears. This is no more the case with a community or nation state than it is with an individual. We have to live with our pasts; but they can be transformed. Thus the British reputation (or is it just an English reputation?) as the rowdy and unpleasant part of a football crowd especially on the continent, comes as little surprise to many Europeans whose experience of us on holiday or as soldiers is of an extremely unsavoury bunch. It is as if we have an attitude, born of long years of imperial power, which we cannot escape and which we will not let go, and which gives us the impression that everyone and everything is there for the taking. Such impressions are real; to become conscious of them hurts our national pride, and undermines our sense of individual identity as a British (or English) person. But taking responsibility for that past will lead to a growth of understanding as to why we should (however wrongly) have behaved in the way we did in the past.

Such perspectives have much to give us as we look at the problems in Northern Ireland, or in the Middle East, or in connection with Iraq and Iran, or the future of the Tamil population in Sri Lanka. Can the historians help us so to understand the past as to give us new opportunity of choosing futures which will enable us to take responsibility for the grim realities which the past shows us? There is no reason why not. That is the implication of our faith in the God and Father of our Lord Jesus Christ.

One way we have of making this point is by way of the doctrine of the incarnation. The whole created order, we claim, is capable of taking the character of the creator himself. Whereas in the Old Testament Moses was permitted only a look at God's back because the glory was too great for the world to take without self-destruction, the New Testament proclaims the presence of God's glory, his very self and character. Furthermore, in this assumption of the character of God, nothing is in principle rejected, for the manner of God's creative activity is redemptive, inclusive, whole and free. So the task to which we are called as ministers and priests is the celebration of God's presence in history, and the attempt to recognize what is going on so that it will be more apparent in ordinary experience as well as in public life. The sacraments point to and offer an opportunity to share in this 'real presence'.

And the Christian community of faith has in history a unique role. Often it has been thought of as an escape, or at the most a byway. There have even been those who have wanted to glorify the church and to regard it as perfection in the sense that it had to keep itself separate from the world in case it was stained by sin. As the saved community of believers, it has been said, that would have been to deny its calling. But these are false hopes, and if true would undermine the faith of Christendom. The church is not the saved community, but the saving community; as such it can only itself know what it is to be in process of being saved, largely through the desire of its members to be so. It shares in the world's sin, as any examination of its history will show. The blind conquest of Mexico for catholicism, or the unfeeling missionary work of contemporary aggressive protestantism in Africa, together with the justification of some of the policies of National Socialism by Kittel or Althaus will convince one of this, quite apart from any scrutiny of the concerns and fears of any local church or individual Christian believer. But that sharing in sin is a necessary condition of the work of the saving community, much as one will regret the consequences of it for the church and for the world.

The role of the church is, therefore, in the light of a vital approach to an understanding of what is taking place historically, to proclaim the presence of God and the hope which flows from that. It is to instantiate and anticipate the kingdom of God. This is a subtle and ever-changing matter. The kingdom is not a state of bliss, but the province of love and hope in the presence of God, Father, Son and Holy Spirit. It therefore implies a set of relationships capable of coming to terms with the tensions, aggressions and fears which dominate the past, because they dominate us. Given that there is the prospect of ultimate fulfilment because of the presence of God eternally, then the encouragement to take seriously the possibility of creatively coping with tensions is paramount. It will need to be stated regularly in worship, in sacrament and in conversation, but it is a reality, and can be witnessed to with confidence. There was a time when the ecumenical movement sought the unity of all churches in one organic model church. That theologically is no doubt what should be sought, since the division of the churches cannot in any sense be affirmed to imply a division in the body of Christ. Yet any chance that there may have been immediately after the Second World War to achieve this desirable end, has been lost as a result of selfishness, fear, misunderstanding, and lack of vision and hope. Yet can we not embrace the experience of failure to achieve unity, and the present uncomfortable fact of division to teach a divided and fearful world how to manage even destructive relationships hopefully and optimistically? If we cannot, who will? Assuredly we will fail to do so if we do not attend with care to the processes of history which have brought us to the present situation, and the even longer processes of God's commitment to us in history which make such optimism realistic. So we are as Christian ministers committed to history and to theology.

Some years ago, we attended to the question, 'What sort of society?' Groups met to discuss what sort of society we wanted, but it was without the benefit of historical analysis, and without awareness of what was going on. Such discussions are without foundation; they breed despair and a desire to protect ourselves from contamination through isolation. Paradoxically respect for the truth, a knowledge of what is happening, and a commitment to take responsibility for the future and the past in the present, is the only basis of hope. It is the gospel. The present anti-intellectualism which includes a profound hostility to the arts in general and to history in particular is anti-Christian.

6
Using Literature as a Theological Resource

Have you read any good books lately? What does the process of reading do to you? Have you read any novels, or poetry, or criticism? Does it matter anyway, since literature is a form of escape, of polite entertainment or vicarious experience? It does matter: literature is none of these. Literature, as Roland Barthes claims, has the aim of putting meaning into the world. And what minister is not concerned to unpack the significance of experience and to bring meaning to the world? If that is what we are involved with, then we cannot ignore writing, especially when taken in association with literary criticism. We need to recognize the importance of oral tradition, and certainly not to reject it, but it is through attention to the written tradition that we shall be in touch with the mainspring of human imagination, feeling and sense.

There was a time when most ministers wrote their sermons before preaching them; we now think differently since what seems important is the immediacy and transparency of what we say. A literary style which is too worked over or too artificial would perhaps interfere with the vitality of personal communication. There is truth in this, though it can be over-emphasized. Too many of the sermons one hears lack either substance or else appear to say things which one knows the preacher would rather not have said. This experience makes clear the vital importance of writing, of taking the time to write oneself and to read what one has written; the sheer physical act of putting things into writing sharpens one's perception of what one is trying to say. The process of putting ideas into written form has an entirely different impact from uttering it in speech, interesting and revealing as that itself can be. A crucial part of this is that the physical material can be seen, touched, it can be felt, it has become an object, a part of the world of experience itself in a way that even recorded speech is not. It can be criticized and evaluated; it can be shaped and revised.

The written story can therefore change one's perception of the world. It is not even the reading of another's story, but the reading of our own that can surprise us as we discover things that we did not know we were trying to say. The text of the story becomes something quite independent of the author, however intimately it may be bound up with his or her autobiographical experience. It is important to grasp this point in relation to pastoral care, and in relation to our own perception of what we are trying to say. Get people to write down what they think they want to say; write down what you think you are trying to say. And above all, read what other people are writing. To work at these things is to share in the changing of the world.

Such a remark may seem to exaggerate; it does not. If anything it understates the importance of all art to the future well-being of society, and certainly it understates the importance of writing and the written word. Art is concerned centrally with the capacity of human beings to be themselves, and certainly to be themselves with others. It was John Austin who referred to facts as slippery, for they come in such a very large number of shapes and sizes. Nevertheless one has to say that they are a sensitive ingredient of what we are talking about here. Writing, and literature are in some sense concerned with the facts. But the perception of facts, the acquisition of new knowledge in the conventional sense of that term is not by any means the most obvious way in which the world is changed. On the contrary, it is feelings, overall apprehension of context, realization of the inner relationship of things, awareness of our role in relation to what we know, recognition of the courses of action that are open to us that change the world. Understanding of what is going on and what could be in relation to what we can do are the things that matter. This is what literature brings to our attention, because it invites participation, sharing, and involvement. To change the world is to recognize that we are and have been involved in a process.

When we write we shape our world and perceive it anew. When we read we share in the creative activity of the artist who

Using Literature as a Theological Resource 79

made what we read, because what has been written is no longer the author's possession, it is given to us to work with, to use, to hold and to shape. Thus both the writer and the reader are themselves shaped by their different relationships with the material which they produce jointly. Participation in its different ways within the production of the object on the part of the writer and reader makes a difference to them both. It changes the world.

Of course there is a sort of use of language which prevents this perspective occurring, and which for example has as its motive utterly non-literary purposes such as the making of money, or the winning of converts. Without wishing to engage in semantics, such use of language is no more literature than its use to train animals or instruct computers. It should not worry us that language can be used in this way, though it should make us as ministers all the more anxious to celebrate literature, and to involve our people through our reading and writing in shaping the truth for themselves. Whatever else literature is, it is not a minor diversion for those who have the leisure to enjoy it; it is a means by which we involve ourselves with the creative edge of human responsibility for God's world and ourselves within it.

The fact is that the Christian religion has a book, the Bible, as a gearbox of engagement with the continuity of reflection on the nature of God and what it is for human beings to be free to act in the world by recognizing the relationship which they have with him. The volume contains a plethora of styles of approach to the grasping, interpreting, and beginning of a conversation about these things. For example, God is celebrated in natural human emotions of victory by poetry and song, but despite the naturalness of these feelings they do not always seem right in relation to those who suffer. And how does that suffering fit the sense that God should be favourably disposed towards those who are obedient to their perception of what he demands, when it is blatantly obvious that he is not? It rains on everyone! All die. But suppose God is a moral being, who wills to effect his purposes in collaboration with all people, and who by his consistency puts the faith of the world to the test? Such a test would not be to catch it out, much less to defeat it, but to bring it opportunities of hope and courage and fulfilment which it would not otherwise have. Furthermore, such faith would have to be instantiated, not simply talked about; it would have to be presented not simply stated. And each of these overlapping and inter-related phases, culminating in the Christian celebration of the story of God in creation and redemption, act and process, narrative and event, is dug over, added to, found alternately stimulating and depressing in the biblical traditions of hope and anxiety offered to the world by the church in our present Bible. Read this, we say, in bits and in large chunks, and tell us what you can see as a result; explore the difference in your life which comes about as a result of reading this volume, and you may rediscover some of the excitement and frustration which those who wrote it, edited it and chose the pieces had in putting it together. All such experience of literature is a beginning and a preparing to begin again. It is not surprising because all knowing is a preparation to learn. One of the tasks of the preacher is to talk us into beginning to talk for ourselves.

But people have to be enticed into a position where they want to give themselves to a relationship, it is not simply second nature. The analogy with human personal relationships is irresistible. We do not just accept people at face value, we need to be wooed; we do not know, on the other hand, what people are like apart from experience of them so we have to commit ourselves to them. Such commitment is a necessary condition of growth for ourselves, since without being open to receive, we shall be in no position to give. That is a paradox for if our giving is to be self-conscious we have to know ourselves, whereas in the vulnerability which comes from opening up ourselves to others, we are as likely to be hurt as treated gently and to realize that we did not know ourselves. So how can we want to take such a risk? Only out of love of truth, and in the confidence which comes from the faith that the truth is lovable because it is loving.

We believe that giving is as blessed as receiving. The experience of human love is paralleled in our experience of a literary text. We come into contact with it, and the writer has to attract us, to nourish our interest, to cajole us into going for a walk with it. It is apparently a thoroughly malleable structure and, to a large extent, that is why so many novels and poems have been used by readers for their own purposes. A reader can be unaffected by the text because the text, like God, leaves us free to make of it what we will. So Jane Austen only wrote romances, James Conrad adventure stories, and D. H. Lawrence sex novels. They can be picked up and put down at will according to our mood, if such is

Using Literature as a Theological Resource 81

the case. But if they are concerned with truth and to engage with it in the company of others then they will be neglected at our peril. What society and companionship with what text has refreshed our desire to wrestle with confusion and perplexity? What do you want to bring others into contact with in order that you can see more clearly yourself what you are about?

Any implication for your understanding of God, or rather what it is to be coming into relationship with him can be left to the end of the chapter, but the God who offers himself to us through the text of his world, is only known through the commitment we offer to make something of ourselves with him. No more than the meaning of the text does God live in his world. However, like meaning in the text God inhabits his world and is apart from it, to be known and to know are both alike parts of the being that we become. God who knows himself can be completely unknown; our growth in knowledge of him requires an acceptance of the fact that we must accept the truth about ourselves through offering to become what we will be through knowledge of him.

The genre of narrative has been of particular recent interest to literary scholars, to theologians, especially biblical scholars, and has also been central to our understanding of meaning. What is a novel if it is not concerned with telling a story? Well, there are other answers to that question, but in a significant sense it is all true; all literature is involved with telling a story. So the excitement of reading *Great Expectations* is to discover what happened to Pip, as Charles Dickens unfolds the story to us. But 'what happened to Pip' is an abbreviation which covers all that involves Pip through background, ability to handle experience, capacity to distance himself from experience and take responsibility for himself; it concerns the gamut of contacts, emotions, friends, hopes and interests, which come his way and which threaten or enhance his ability to see what the choices are that he can make. And in the reading of the novel, it is not that we vicariously share in experiences which are not ours, nor that we are simply having a good read though it is to be hoped that we are, rather through the reading of the novel we are taken into a possibility of self-discovery. There is the opportunity of refreshment.

Time is central to this experience, and in many ways. The length of a novel is a matter of fine judgment, it has to be just right for the subject matter. Thus Proust was right to think (though I do not believe he knew before he had started writing) a novel on memory and the power of memory to recreate and to entrap would need to be long. The convoluted and entrancing world of our past, which alike enchains and enlivens our present and future, comes both in brief images and in deep waves of meaning. Thus too the novel *Remembrance of Things Past*, covering some forty years and filling eight volumes, (twelve in the English translation) takes such time to be read as might enable us to grasp its central point that the past is always with us to surprise, direct and re-interpret our present and future. On the other hand, Saul Bellow's early novel *Dangling Man* is only some 150 pages, covering a period of four months during which a man seeks the freedom he knows he will lose when the date for his call-up to military service arrives. The freedom he finds is a prison he has made for himself; he cannot wait for it to end in the pattern and structure of disciplined life which denies him necessarily the responsibility he would not and could not accept for himself.

Time is also relevant in respect of the period in which the novel is set. William Golding's *The Inheritors* is not an historical novel, but its universality is determined by its prehistoric setting. The same might be said of David Hughes' *The Pork Butcher* whose contemporary setting awakens one to the possibility of reconciliation and the need of it. And when was the story written? That too can be significant. J. G. Ballard's *Empire of the Sun* must be one of the most sensitive accounts of childhood that we have, written partly from personal experience in the China of the Second World War and the prison camp environment. But apart from the literary merits which are many, one must also point to the time when the book was written, 1984. Many people seem to think we are under threat as a human race; we may survive as living creatures, but will our humanity grace the world with affection and joy? The ingenious humanity of Jim, excited by new experience, involved with death and violence in a disintegration of everyday society, nevertheless emerges as deeply human. He is no martyr, no paragon of virtue, or hell-care survivalist; he is human, he is Jim. The context for the reading of the story is always there, but it happened consciously or unconsciously to be recognized.

All these stories gather up bits of us as we read them, so that we move along in their company. We are acted on by them, and act upon them. The story is not just there in the text, it is what we make it. And we must make room for the critic, not too much room, but enough. I say not too much room, because the critic who draws attention to the text appropriately is the one to be emphasized, not the critic who uses the text to support his own theory or personality. Too many examination papers give evidence of ability to remember what the critics have said, when what we want to know is the capacity of the student to grapple with and be open to the text. But there are critics one wants to know and to read because in their writing they give evidence of the enchantment and re-creation of walking with certain texts. They help us to take account of the time which might otherwise blind us to the humanity of a writer. Thus Douglas Brown persuaded me to read George Herbert, and Raymond Brown the Gospel of St. John, and Roland Barthes just to go on reading.

Could there be necessary stories? Stories which are as much a feature of being human as having a skeleton and being hirsute? Perhaps there are stories which it constitutes deprivation not to have been involved with. For example, they may be stories which have been so much a feature of human experience that if we are not familiar with them we lose touch with the past and lack the ability to find our position in the world. It could hardly be that they had to be the same stories literally for each person for we should then be involved with the difficulties of natural language and the problems of translation. Neither could it be the case that involvement with the stories would have to produce the same reactions in each person if the story was to be regarded as effective. But without exposure to literature, to the distillation of human enquiry and the hope that it contains, there is little chance that a person will begin to tell his own story, and without that one might say that he or she does not exist. But then if we are to learn to tell our own story we must come to terms with the fact of existence, with the implications of its temporality and accidental nature, with its mysterious random position in the world of space and time, and with the threat and delightful necessity of other people if we are to be ourselves. To the extent that the apprehension of the importance of these questions and the ability to deal with them is raised by certain structures of story and stimulates certain stories, we must regard it as a matter of worthwhile enquiry that there could be essential stories for our humanity. The pervasiveness of religion, mythology and literature would suggest that there is some evidence already. We might even want to argue that the attempt by the Christian gospel to grasp and to tell the story of the love affair of God with the world was one such story. But what is that story? How do we tell it? How do we engage with it?

It is often said that every person has a least one novel in them. It is certainly true that each of us has at least one autobiography in him or her. The trouble is just that. We have to decide which of the possible autobiographies to tell in our lives. We could have a complete image of the person we were and live out our lives according to a preconceived notion of exactly how such a person will behave in every circumstance. Scholars have often led us to believe that this was what was in the mind of the Jewish lawyers of the time of Jesus, or the Roman Catholic moralists of the nineteenth century. At least they understood what it was to be a human being of a particular type and attempted to deduce the appropriate behaviour to fulfil the ideal. But this is no real help: people are not like that. Most people do not know who they are, are blinded to their own natures, and cultivate illusions. Given choices therefore they are not simply perplexed about what they should do, they are perplexed about what could be done. Our lives are much more apparently like blank pieces of paper on which we have to write, than they are like those paint-by-numbers pictures. And that's the difficulty. Any writer will admit that the actual beginning is always fraught with danger. To sit in front of a virgin sheet of paper and to make a mark on it is to begin what I cannot know whether I will finish. Indeed, it is to begin what I do not know how to finish. Nor do I know what will come between the beginning and the end, because the actual writing changes what was going to come, even if when I started I thought I knew. The writer is always puzzled and anxious about whether he will be able to manage the beast that is coming to be through the creative act of writing. And so are we in regard to the ordinary business of living. Much better not to take the risk of beginning, or to take down somebody else's life from the shelf and to try and live that, or perhaps to live somebody else's life for him or her. Anything rather than take responsibility for our own life, especially since that means getting to know other people and going through the problems of coping with the unforseen.

But we cannot avoid it. We have responsibility for ourselves,

Using Literature as a Theological Resource 85

however much we might wish to qualify that in the light of experience, and attention to the work of historians and scientists for example. No manner of increase in such knowledge removes this responsibility, as is implicit in the Genesis story of the fall. Knowledge does not imply fall into sin, especially if by sin there is implied any sense of guilt. On the other hand, reliance on knowledge does not remove the fact of human responsibility; the fact is that its increase awakens in us a new sense of responsibility. Of course we may not like that and may seek to hide our humanity behind expertise or skills. But it never works. Society does not need more scientists or technologists at the moment, though many would lead us to think that the economy would improve if we had them in train loads. What we need is more people who, alongside all their human perceptions, intriguing capacity for relationships and educated expectations, are capable of taking responsibility for their science and technology. More people like that would be splendid, because they would be aware of the acquisition of responsibility with their knowledge. Experience of and participation in literature is crucial to the acquisition of the skill to tell our story, to be responsible for our knowledge, to be ourselves. We write our lives, though they cannot be written alone, if they are to be true.

The analogies employed within the Christian tradition are illuminating in the way they lend support to what lies at the heart of this chapter. God creates through his word; it is Jesus Christ the word of God through whom redemption is offered, and by whom atonement is made; it is the Holy Spirit that guides us into all truth, and which therefore enables us to make creative interpretations of our experience.

God is the author of the world. He is engaged on the creation of a text and although he is responsible for it, in the sense that he is the sole author, he cannot determine the meaning. The meaning has to emerge through co-operation with those for whom the world, the text, is prepared. At one time it may have been sensible to think that the part of the text which had meaning had already been completed. As if the total meaning of the universe was revealed during a segment of the world's existence in space-time, and that all humanity had to do was to find out that meaning and remember it in association with appropriate ritual and moral behaviour. This does not seem sensible to us now. Of course humanity may have found some things more revealing or more encouraging than others, and that experience is worth reporting to encourage the rest of us. But that empirical discovery, if it is a fact, is only a fact of human experience, not an objective fact of history or a fact regarding the actual presence of God in the world. On the contrary, we are better to think of God working at his world in the way that an author works on his material; the author has to be attentive to the beginning, concerned to respond to the way the story goes, and conscious of the limits to the malleability of the material if the characters are not to appear unbelievable or the language distorted. It is a dangerous and risky task on which the author is engaged. It is a dangerous and risky task to which God is committed.

Humanity is co-author with God of the world which is coming to be. And this underlines the very riskiness of the operation in which God is engaged. He has fellow actors in the scheme of things. There are readers of his text. Indeed their fulfilment is the aim of the exercise in which he is engaged. And this raises difficult questions about God's authority. Since it is an authority which has to be consistent with the purpose of fulfilling the lives of his co-creators, there is excluded the possibility of their destruction when things go wrong. And this is even more the case when it is their fault when things go that way. So the question arises whether in this demanding relationship, God is in such full knowledge of himself and of the world that he has power over himself to go on giving himself to the world despite its behaviour and condition. So when the story is taken in a direction other than that which might have originally occurred to the author, the question is whether he or she can manage himself or herself in relation to that change, or whether frustration and disappointment lead to ripping it up, putting it in the wastepaper basket and starting again. You have got to like writing, to understand the process, and to like the actual material with which you are wrestling, to want to go on working at it. What Christians say about God is that that condition represents the position of God in relation to the world. He likes creating, and is devoted to the well-being of the particular thing which he is making now; he loves it in fact.

But humanity does not find it easy to accept this. In like manner with God, as co-creator, we find the material with which we are dealing not malleable in the ways in which we think it should go.

As individuals, classes, families, nations, races, we believe that the world is in fact stacked against us. Most particularly we believe that other people are stacked against us, and that since we cannot see how to go on working with them, the only solution is to wipe them off the face of the earth. We find it difficult to accept any change of direction in the story we want to tell of our lives, and so we will not adjust to circumstances, or learn from experience. The pain which this brings is often terrifying in terms of broken relationships, lost hopes and self-destruction. But in prospect, it seems preferable to a change of direction which we can often dress up in terms of loss of principles. Happily God has no principles of that external definitive kind. But even that humanity can see as betrayal, as if freedom without the risk of commitment was a real possibility. And whereas what humanity looks for is the exercise of external authority to make the story come out as we had attempted to predetermine it, what God offers is authoritativeness, the encouragement of his presence so that the story can continue co-operatively to be written in love.

So God is not only related to the world in an external way, he is himself wholly committed to it and intends to see it through to the end. That is what Christians affirm in their reflection upon the work and nature of Jesus whom we call the Christ. God does not say in the word of his creating, 'Here is the physical world, and here are the instructions for the way you must behave in it,' and then keep constant check on us to see how we are climbing the snakes and going down the ladders! On the contrary, since he depends upon us if his world is to be real, he has to show us that he is worth trusting, worth working with, and that the world itself is capable of being grappled with in the interests of human being. That is what Christians in their story-telling about Jesus and their reflection on his life in relation to its background in Judaism were forced to conclude about God himself. He will never give up his authorship. Nor will he ever deny that he made the world; rather he will go on wanting to give himself to us in order that the story we are writing can constantly be made meaningful.

And that is not a conclusion but a further beginning. For God does not in Jesus Christ bring all things to an end, as if at last we have got the authority to say, 'do this . . .'. What we are required to do is to accept the risk of living and working with him. That is why the reflection of St John's gospel is so crucial and so encouraging. The Spirit which is sent by the Son will lead us into all truth. Truth for the Hebrew was at least as much concerned with the real experience of a living relationship as it was with the discovery of objective truths. And this is what we find. When the business of working at the story ourselves becomes, as it does from time to time at least, more than we can bear, it is the pulse of the living God present in all things which can convince us that the story is still capable of development. The text remains, and God the author. What is more, although the changes may be dramatic, when compared with how we thought it should go at one time, when we read the whole thing through from the beginning, there is a coherence and pattern which gives us increasing ability to go on making sense of our experiences. Faith therefore gives us grounds of hope. It is a principle with which we have to reckon that not everything can be fitted in. Furthermore, in any selection things are excluded as well as included. The art of the historian is to choose just those circumstances, conditions, events and persons to give a sufficiently clear and characteristic account of what is going on. The art of the writer in any literary genre is to select creatively. Certainly in relation to the telling of our own story, in the life which we live, to attempt everything would be to achieve nothing and to make no sense of anything. Two interesting features of Christian theology emerge here, the doctrines of incarnation and sin.

To select creatively is to identify those features of a story which make it possible for it to go on being told. In our reading we all too frequently find a novel or a poem or a play which it is difficult to go on reading. One of the reasons is often that too much has been included for us to get the hang of the thing; and certainly too much for us to be involved with what we are reading. But equally, crucial things cannot be left out; if the thread is missing we are unable to hold things together. The writer and the reader have to be able to work at what they have. The art of living is in an analogous category. We make choices of career, of friendship, of books to read, and from these choices together with the events which perforce come our way, we construct the story of our lives. In Christian terms, we do it in the light of a conviction that persons can commit themselves wholly to the world and not be overcome by it but encouraged and sustained by it. To succeed in such an aim is to share in the incarnation which is presented by God in

Using Literature as a Theological Resource 89

Christ. But even that fulfilment is only a beginning, as the pattern of the life of Christ himself suggests.

Having the courage to choose is hard, having the courage to let go is probably much more difficult. On this fact rests the power of sin. So the regret and failures live with us as constant reminders of defeat and anxiety. They are frequently nourished and sustained, as if they are the very things which give us our identity and present us as different from all others. Now such events are not simply to be forgotten. The psychoanalist has at least convinced us that the past lives with us to influence and direct, so that what we are not reconciled to will with effortless potency threaten our capacity to grow and make sense of our lives always. But the analogy of literature helps again. The selection of what to give credence to, where to put our hope in our experience, is like the ability of the author to select in order to be able to go on telling the story. Events which are significant can be left out, though their impact will be built into the story and assumed in what occurs. So in any subtle study of character in a novel the events in the early chapters will be present in their effects on the person and the situation through to the end, though only some will be seen to be the ones that are determinative. Forgiveness is the condition which enables us to take account of our past responsibly and to handle it creatively; it gets things in proportion and keeps them so, though it will appear in the course of our story that aspects of our lives come and go in importance. The possibility that we can get and keep things in just such creative proportion depends upon our awareness of the authoritativeness of God, and the sense that we have of the continuing commitment he has to the success of what he has begun. With that assurance we can live with ourselves, know the power of forgiveness, and the ever-present possibility of resurrection. The story we have begun can take a new direction and live.

The trouble is that we have the impression that a written text is unchangeable. Nothing could be further from the truth. Time will extend the story and transform its meaning; the interpreter will, in the light of his own experience, bring new perspectives to bear. The reader may himself or herself begin to accept responsibility for the work of art. God and humanity may do likewise in respect of their mutual commitment to the world: for it is a creation.

And the minister wrestles with the incarnating of this reality and does so by directing attention to God, the author of all things.

7
Community Wisdom

The minister is the theological resource person in the Christian community. It has been the theme of this book to underscore the fact that no minister can be this for others within the community unless there is commitment to the task on the part of the minster personally. How can we direct the attention of others to God unless we are trying to focus on him ourselves? The image is appropriate, for since we can never describe what we see in God with sufficient accuracy or completeness to exhaust the love and truth to be found in him, the description which we give can never be a substitute for God himself as others may see him. Furthermore, the incompleteness of our own vision requires the insights of others. Those insights are not simply necessary because there are more points on the scale than we can see, or because others have different light filtered out, but because the perspective we have for ourselves will be inclined to lack balance, and to encourage prejudice. In the same way as in any other human enquiry, so also in theology, the task on which we are engaged is a task for the whole community.

But it needs a point of reference, and that can most constructively be the minister or priest. And in this, as in other respects, the minister is representative of the community. Hence the education of the minister must introduce the best information possible in all the areas that have been discussed here and above all provide sufficient experience of the celebration of the gospel in sacrament and liturgy, for the bare bones of the action of God's involvement with the world to be a regular spring of spiritual nourishment and hope. It is the celebration of that activity most expecially in the eucharist which provides the stimulus for the preaching which attempts to build the congregation into the conversation about the meaning and reality of God for the world, and for each of them. Such a responsibility requires careful and attentive reflection if it is genuinely to direct attention to God, and to validate the experience of the hearer, rather than de-skill him or her by directing attention to the preacher.

So we come into the presence of God without anything other than ourselves. And we are accepted by the creator whose redemptive purpose is potentially fulfilled by his knowledge of himself and his utter willingness to give himself. In that presence we can grow in knowledge of ourselves, and have the confidence to make our confession. God's presence is the condition of our confession, not the consequence of it; God's grace is, as we say, prevenient. The declaration of forgiveness is the affirmation of a state of affairs; our sins are forgiven. In this new awareness of the state in which we are truly ourselves, the scriptures are read, beginning with the explorations and perplexities of the Old Testament, the joy of the first Christians in the epistle, and concluding with the foundation and root of our faith in the reading of the gospel. This developing conversation of humanity with God, to which we are thus introduced, is to be continued in the preaching as the meaning of it all is wrestled with through the experience of the preacher and an awareness of the context in which that meaning is sought. The key is that just as the subsequent celebration of God's presence in the eucharist is not a private or individualist activity, so neither is that preaching. The preacher is not trying to impose his word on the congregation, but to excite their interest in thinking, and learning to make sense of things for themselves. And above all it must lead the preacher to listen to his congregation so that he can find meaning in what he is saying.

This is hard to learn, for the tendency is to presume that since he has the knowlege he has the truth. And, of course, if he has the truth, he has not only the right but the duty to try and impose it on the rest of the world. Such a view of truth is utterly misleading. Quite apart from whether it is true that all ministers do have the knowledge that would be requisite, the truth of God which we share and celebrate, should enliven a sense of responsibility, not a sense of power. Far from implying that the truth is known and can now be imposed to the benefit of all, it should make us aware of new opportunities of response-ability. Such opportunities come because potentially at least we have, in the light of our real but meagre knowledge, the ability to listen more carefully to what others are saying and to engage freely with them in the pursuit of truth. We are able more completely to celebrate what others know because we possess our own knowledge more lightly. The more we know, the more we realize we want to know, and the greater we recognize our involvement to be with others in knowing anything. But whether we can accept this depends, not only upon the extent of our knowledge of the world outside us, but the depth of our knowledge of ourselves.

The point I am making is analogous to that made by Harry Williams in his discussion of poverty. Poverty is the condition which enables us to possess all things, whether they actually belong to us or not. So if a friend has a garden full of the most delightful flowers and shrubs, we can take the greatest pleasure in their beauty of form and arrangement – even if we have no prospect of owning such a garden ourselves. Our lack of possessiveness frees us to appreciate and enjoy everything. That capacity has to develop in us in respect of knowledge. It is a temptation to take our identity from what we know, as if we were constituted of all that we knew. Of course, if we were so constituted, to give knowlege away, or even to share it, would be to diminish ourselves. But the contrary is the case, in order to know what we think we know, in order really to possess it, we have to give it away, even if by so doing we discover that we had hold of the wrong end of the stick all the time. Only in the light of such experience of giving have we the opportunity to gain the new knowledge which comes from receiving. We rely on other people even to know the meaning of what we know, let alone to extend the range of our knowledge.

So in learning to speak the truth it is necessary that we celebrate the truth which others possess. This has many dimensions to it, and is a hard thing to accept. On the face of it, it is easy because it is perfectly obvious that we do not know everything; but in fact it is very difficult. After all, the truth we have is so valuable and so vulnerable, we hardly dare to expose it, let alone accept that others have truth too. But it is not just the personal dimensions of the problem, there are other features of the situation which require work if we are to rescue our lives from prejudice and ineffectuality. I mention three contexts, the past, other religions, and atheism. I choose these three because they provide the context of our exploration and therefore contribute to our exploring. The past is not separate from us, but contains us; its riches store and make available wisdom beyond our experience which enables us to understand what is wise about the present exploring of Christian faith. Other religions celebrate the search for reality and anchor Christian experience in the concrete reality of all human enquiring. Atheism only exists in a sense because of the uniqueness of the revelation which has been claimed by Christian believers, its insights are part of the same thrust for truth. Christian wisdom is based in the human experience informed and structured and stimulated by the reflection of the community of faith in the light of the life of Christ. First, the past.

To read the Church Fathers is to involve oneself in a world which appears foreign to us. It is so foreign indeed that we project our inability to understand them into a presumption that they did not really understand the faith, let alone the world in which they found themselves. We fondly imagine that our generation has made such strides in both of these contexts that they have now nothing to offer us, though of course it can be quaint and amusing to browse amongst their extraordinary views. But the truth is that it is our fear of finding our own age, our own theology to be incomplete that distorts our ability to get to grips with the truth as they perceived it. It was the willingness of Wesley and Pusey to attend to their insights that led to the radical movements in the church of Methodism and the Oxford Movement. It was the theology of Irenaeus which, when placed alongside that of St Augustine, filtered through a generous and perceptive mind which gave us the marvellous *Evil and the God of Love* by John Hick; it is the powerful reflections of Gregory of Nyssa which lie behind our attempts to find a theology to inform the ecological crisis. The truth is that any theologian pursues the truth as he sees it, and proclaims the God in whom he hopes. On their witness, and in their society, we build our own perspective. No more can we afford to neglect conversation with them, than with the thinkers of our own time. And on whom can we depend to point us in that direction if not the theologically-aware minister? For it is his vocation to be with all those who love God in every generation.

The same point should be made about spirituality most particularly. The faith has had many giants of the spiritual life, and we shall be foolish indeed if we drink the *vin nouveau* of the last twenty years and remain ignorant of the matured wine of the centuries. To have at our disposal the treasury of spiritual classics from St Augustine, Abelard, St John of the Cross, Fenelon, de Caussade, The Cloud of Unknowing, Newman as well as the solid contributions of the twentieth century is essential if the Christian community is to grow through finding its roots. No one needs them all, but everyone needs something, and again who will help us to remain in touch with the whole range of Christian devotion if not the minister? As others have focused their attention on God, so may we.

The Christian community has, particularly in its ecclesiatical and institutional form, been extremely introspective and internalized. Fear of losing out has led us to look only to ourselves for encouragement and for celebration of the reality of God. Such fear is dangerous, unrealistic and a complete misunderstanding of the wild generosity of God in his giving. So we have to accept that the community of faith which has its roots and its tradition, itself operates amongst a community of joy and enquiry in which the reality of God is apparent to those who have eyes to see, and who are prepared to put in the sort of work which is necessary. Thus painters, sculptors, landscape designers, architects, poets, engravers, playwrights, novelists, creative artists, all offer the possibility of insight which incarnates more of the reality of God in the story of our lives. And other religions too, though we seem to have found this particularly difficult to accept. And even when we have accepted it intellectually, we have still not been able to take the sort of steps which would enable us to be true to ourselves and our vision of God, when we open up ourselves to the experience presented in the lives of, say, Jewish or Buddhist believers. But this we have to do.

The Old Testament, we have to say, is not the preliminary work of God in preparing for the gospel in the New Testament; it is first and foremost the holy book, the scripture of the Jewish people. No understanding of its literature will enable one to get inside it; therefore, since it is the book which so informs and illuminates the New Testament, we shall not understand that until we are in relationship with Judaism. Yet the recognition of the Jewish community of faith as a religious and moral embodiment of hope in God with all the consequences which flow from that, has not been a central feature of Christian enquiring or faith. Indeed, the contrary is the case, with anti-semitism encouraged by a dogmatism which owes nothing to truth and everything to fear.

It is not of course that there are no differences of perception of Judaism and Christianity, as if when Jews see what Christians are saying they will all realize that they are Christians really. Rather, it is because there are real, important and potentially fascinating differences in our various perceptions of God that we need to converse, and widen our community of enquiry to encompass them. Such a change of relationship will hardly be easy given the suspicion, the social and economic experience which each has of the other, and the political reductionism which is always inclined to overtake each tradition. But when we set our attention on God, and recognize that this is what in principle each of us has done and wants to do, then in mutual commitment we have the prospect of becoming more ourselves as we grow in knowledge of him. If in the end we do have to admit that we are part of the same tradition of enquiry, and that our differences do not matter, it will be as a result of the activity of God, not our persuasiveness, or our astute calculation of political advantage.

The Buddhist tradition is more difficult. Whereas when it comes to recognizing the sense and seriousness of Jewish seeking for God, we at least have the misleading illusion that there is such a thing as the Judaeo-Christian tradition, when we look at Buddhism it seems alien and even non-religious. Whereas, for example, the Christian religion lays emphasis upon the person, and the fulfilment of his or her being in mutual relationship with God, the Buddhist would regard such a faith as illusory since such a sense of personal identity lies behind the pain and frustration which is part and parcel of human life in this world. So when Christians look to heaven as the context of salvation, they see its attraction in terms of fulfilled personal identity through life constantly renewed in relation to God, but the Buddhist on the contrary looks to Nirvana as that state of blissful absorption of the one in the all, and the cessation of all self-regard and self-identity. But when did the recognition of difference of approach to what it is to be a human being necessitate loss of contact, or refusal of relationship? The very differences are illuminating. Furthermore, even a modest familiarity with the insights and aspirations of Buddhism, will lead one to recognize that, as with Christianity, there are many schools of thought, many traditions of worship, a very human approach to moral concern, especially for the non-human world, and many continuing developments in the twentieth century.

For many Christians, atheism offers the most questionable range of traditions. Even those who can celebrate the insights of other religious traditions, and see them as part of the community of enquiry into the nature and reality of God, often cannot see the same with regard to atheism. Here are the people opposed in principle to the very reality of God which the rest of us take seriously. Can there be any response other than opposition? Personal scorn is hard to take lightly; political opposition offers a threat to institutional Christianity in many countries; on both counts therefore it is important to distinguish between the religious, philosophical and moral issues which are at stake here, and the often misleading structures in which they can be found. After all we would not wish the seriousness of our religious intuitions and reflections to be confused with, let alone identified with, the political or personal prejudices of seventeenth century Europe or the razmataz of the very vocal 'silent majority'. We should not therefore force the deep questioning of devout atheism out of our minds by identifying it with the ignorant prejudices of party officials or even the everyday assumptions of ordinary believers. All of us have to take into account the reality of the question, 'Is there a God?'. Granted that most of us will want to approach it first in qualitative or existential rather than ontological terms, the ontological question is a real one. I say qualitative or existential because the Bible itself approaches the question of the existence of God in this way: it is concerned with his nature and reality, and only therefore secondarily with his existence. What is God like? Is he worth worshipping? Have you a sense of the reality of God for you, and what does that mean? These are some of the questions that the Bible pays attention to. But while these questions are still important, we also have to wrestle with the open-ended question, 'Is there a God?'.

We simply have to see it as a religious question to understand how central it is to our enquiring as Christians. The unity which we give to God, a unity brought to light and emphasized in the Christian tradition by the doctrine of the Trinity, means that the question is a peculiarly Christian one. In a powerful sense it is Christianity which provides the context in which the atheistic question is shaped and can be discussed. If we do not take the question of atheism seriously therefore, others find it hard to do so. Other religious traditions either have no duty to involve the world in theological conversation or if there is an obligation to convert are inclined to do it through opposition rather than shared enquiry. Only Christianity with its desire for universal community and a commitment to the exploration of God as unity, yet both present with and separate from his world, has the duty and opportunity to include atheism within its enquiring conversation. It is all the more sad, therefore, that we should so lamentably fail in this regard, and resort to the language of sociology and psychology, of politics and economics to explain away the need to take seriously the religious insights which we are offered.

In all these matters the minister has the daunting task of being the theological resource person, of admitting his interest, the seriousness of the questions, and his ignorance in dealing with them. In all these contexts he or she has the responsibility of pointing to God and focusing his attention on him. He or she has to learn to speak the truth by learning to celebrate the truth of others. And that can be hard: indeed it should be. The minister's work requires, therefore, that he or she should be willing to remember, anxious to be creative with, and capable of living affectionately with the traditions of Christian faith. The community wisdom is called to mind, made creatively available, and reconciled in this activity. The focus on God is all-inclusive.

Remembering

The personal worlds which we are involved with include the mass of everyday occurrences which demand our attention, the formal ties which bind us into the community of family and faith, of work and leisure interests; and the hidden areas of unconscious influence which emerge from time to time like phantoms from the murky darkness of the sea. The story we are telling with our lives brings coherence to this pattern, and enables us to make choices for the future which can transform our past. Remembering offers the possibility of cultivating the story, of being able to recognize continually who we are, and to draw on the life-giving contexts which sustain and make sense of what we are. It is no different with the faith. We are a set of worlds which include the totality of present experience, the formal ties which hold us together and which also divide us; we are our ways of behaving and worshipping, of praying and thinking about God, of enjoying ourselves and being serious; and it also includes the dark influences which loom from the deep and threaten to shatter us by their uncontrollable power. The story which the Christian faith tells of God's love affair with the world, enables us to bring coherence to this diversity, to live it out in practice, and make choices which enable us to go on telling the story in such a way that the past can be continually transformed and renewed. Ministers are theological resource persons who hold, make available, and attend to the community wisdom.

One of the exciting things about remembering is the realization that what has been remembered was in fact already known. Edwin Muir tells of his conversion to Christianity in his autobiography as occurring when he was putting his trousers on which coincided with his realization that he had been a Christian for some time without knowing it. The prodigal son came to himself when he remembered his father, and the community of life with which he was associated and with which he believed he could no longer pretend he was disassociated. And this process is one which the minister might well remember himself; it may cause him grief as well as joy. For as the person within the community whose task is to remember, and to 'cause others to recall to mind', there can be no surprise if he is not immediately seen as the one with the gimmicky and off-beat ideas, or the one whose bright new truth is the talk of the town. For the majority of the time it will be a matter of reminding people of what they know already. And given that this is the case, the fact that much of what we need to remember, we are for various reasons trying to forget, it will obviously not be surprising if the minister finds himself marginalized. That may be a personal sadness from time to time, but far from bringing to mind the need to find new gimmicks or influence, it should encourage the task of remembering and focusing attention on God. The story must be told again with the fullest awareness of the contexts in which it has been told, which have influenced it, and which are now perhaps capable of influencing it anew or for the first time, in the hope and the belief that the conversation of faith will begin.

For example, hitherto the Christian story has been told with one assumption that patripassionism is a heresy; it was so clearly misleading to think along these lines that it was forbidden to take the thought seriously. Suffering was the experience of Jesus Christ, the Son, the redeemer, the word, through whom all things were made, but not of God the Father, the creator by whom all things were made. Yet in telling the story of the Christian gospel in the twentieth century, there have been many suggestions that there may be an incompleteness in our perception of the nature of God's commitment of himself to his world if we leave out of account the idea of a suffering God. It is not that we have wanted simply to say these sorts of things because on reflection these have looked sensible things if we want converts, but rather given the bitter sense of betrayal from which mankind suffers through the appalling evil and suffering of the world, on reflection and giving attention to God as we are now stimulated to conceive him, these are things we want to say about him. We might want to use the relatively orthodox language of a Pannenberg, or the sharper perceptions of a Moltmann, or the even wider perspectives of John Cobb and the school of process theology, but what we are after is a way of saying the Christian story which does justice to the tradition and to the present experience of life which goes with being human in the twentieth century. The concern of the liberation theologians, and the revived interest in the doctrine of the Trinity alike bear witness to this same fact.

To remember is not to reminisce, but to be alive to the opportunities and needs of the present, through consciousness of the achievements and resources of the past. It is also, most crucially, to be able to forget and forgive ourselves for what has already been forgiven. Some lumber should be discarded.

Creativity

Theology is what the Christian community gets up to; it is not the activity of individuals, still less of private individuals! That is why the minister is always wanting to point to the mass of Christian reflection and to the contexts which make sense of it. But in doing this it is important that no encouragement is given to the view that he is the only person in the community who is thinking theologically, or even more disastrously, who is capable of thinking theologically. As any sensitive appreciation of our conversation will show, we can and do learn from everybody and anybody. It is of the essence of any teaching relationship that the teacher should see that if he or she is not actually learning through the experience of teaching, then the supposed learner will certainly not be either. All teaching is a reciprocal process. The truth is expressed in the heart of the gospel in the way in which Christians talk of the relationship between God and the world as incarnation. Unless God was capable of showing himself to be a learner, he would have forfeited the right, as well as the possibility, of being a teacher. His authority comes from the fact that he identifies himself with that to which he has committed himself. There is no sense in which God can be thought of as creator apart from recognizing him to be redeemer.

But the analogy should not be pressed too far, for there is one absolutely crucial distinction. Whereas God creates *ex nihilo*, thus indicating that in the last resort all responsibility is his, we mere human beings only create by building with what already is. We do not originate in the technical sense. So as ministers we confirm the experience of others, by talking with them, bringing them into such close contact with the traditions of faith and hope in Christ, that they confirm or reject their own experience themselves. We do not tell them the truth, for the truth cannot in that sense be told; we, through conversation of a theological nature and through mutual celebration of the gospel of Christ, may enable them to find the truth for themselves. This maieutic function is a *sine qua non* of our own growth in the faith. The world does not consist of people like us – unless we believe that we have the whole of the truth already divulged to us. None of us can think that with any seriousness, though our behaviour may all too frequently lead others to think that it is what we believe. But none of us is an artist, a writer, a scientist, a doctor, a plumber, a pilot, a builder, a lawyer, a mother, a grandparent, a teacher, a botanist, a gardener, though all of us are called to be aware of the fact that the world has need of each of these forms of human activity, and many of them represent ways of living that each of us will have to try to perform at some stage or other in our lives. Each of these activities, if it is a genuine calling, will have its own truth, its own perspective, its own language, its own relationships; each will therefore have a significance for theological enquiry that it is our task to celebrate, to confirm and to draw on for the benefit of all. Each of them, since it offers something that the community needs, is valued by God who therefore gives himself to it; each of them must be valued by us. Our creativity finds expression in the formation of the world of hope and joy in which the community of faith, and through it, that wider community of humanity, is confirmed.

Loving

The problem is that so many, even of those of the household of faith, seem to be such unlovely people. We do not need, I suppose, to be particularly honest or clear-thinking to recognize that there are large portions of the human race, let alone large numbers of Christians, whose company we would not much enjoy and whose society we would certainly not seek. One comment which is helpful is that God apparently does not expect us either always to enjoy one another's company (and certainly not to say we do when we don't), nor does he actually require us to find ourselves always in the company of those whom we find most antipathetic.

But we are required to be careful how we make these judgments. For example, John Wesley does not seem to have been the most endearing of characters, his autocratic temperament and personal failures of relationship made him a complex and difficult man. But we should be foolish indeed if we allowed that to shut our minds to the qualities of energy and wholeness that he brought to British religious life in the eighteenth century. Furthermore, our failure to appreciate his fine contribution may stem as much from weakness in ourselves as from faults in him. We need to be careful. The same may be true of our present colleagues and any of those with whom we are in fact called to work. Their attitudes may upset us, not because they have not got a point but because we cannot see it. And in order to have a chance of coming to see it, there is just one necessary condition – that of love; we have to love the world of human beings.

Love comes in all shapes and sizes, but clearly what is meant here is that virtue of Christian love, which is concerned with the ultimate well-being of each person, because only by that process can the well-being of all be sought. If it is true, as I believe it is, that as Proudhon said, 'No man is free until all men are free,' then it is equally true that we cannot in the Christian sense of love learn to love any person creatively, until all people are loved. We cannot therefore be in completely the right relationship with anyone until all people are in right relationships with each other. That is a tall order, and if one is not careful, a recipe for despair. But this need not be so if we remember and tell the story of the fullness of God's perfect relationship with all that is. By focusing our attention upon him in his triune nature of creator, redeemer, and encourager we shall find increasing resources on which to draw. Thus we shall gain the freedom to confirm others in the reality of their own selves, as we grow in the knowledge of our own confirmation by God. Thus, and only thus, does the community wisdom of our faith become free of the party strife, personal ambition, human misunderstanding and blindness which so characterizes its current presentation. It can be done: it is being done.

This is a high calling, and requires a celebration of the distinctive nature of Christian prayer and worship; and so it is to the world of things, and people and the celebration of God's presence with us that we now finally turn. And our hope rests in the knowledge that the truth is lovable, and in that sense always knowable and available. That is, if we want God we already know him. To remember that is to possess all things.

8
Addressing God

The principal aim of this book is to review what Christian ministry is fundamentally about, and to suggest that its distinguishing mark, its source and its end, is to focus on God. This focus on God distinguishes ministry from social work, and the church from a club. The good news about God is what mission proclaims, however unwilling our contemporaries may be to hear the message. If it is not true then we do not deserve to convince. The minister's task is to nurture and facilitate discernment of God, response to him, and the positive shouldering of responsibility in his world.

The task belongs not just to the ordained minister, but to the whole local Christian community, and the whole community shares in it. The minister is the leader and guide of a party on an expedition. Some tasks will be delegated. The welfare of the whole group will depend upon the vision and collaboration of all its leaders. The minister will not be the only map-reader, and others may be responsible for organizing the necessary provisions. Someone, however, needs to have acquaintance with the terrain, and the pitfalls that have diverted other expeditions. It is not that former expeditions provide us with ready made answers, but they do sometimes save us making unprofitable digressions. Someone needs to keep the group from getting ingrown and insular, and becoming so concerned about immediate problems that the ultimate goal dims. Leadership needs to be focused in someone, and that someone is likely to be the one we regard as the representative person, the ordained minister. It is his job to foster the church's theological self-awareness, and prevent it stagnating.

It is primarily in the context of worship that this nurturing takes place. There is no escape from the fact that leading the church's worship lies at the heart of the ministerial task. Something has already been said about the preaching responsibility. But there is also the responsibility for praying. We should never underestimate the extent to which theological understanding is fostered or distorted by the public praying of the church, nor should we imagine that private spirituality can be divorced from theological awareness and reflection if the praying is to be true to the Christian tradition. It is to these areas that we turn in this final chapter.

Praying both public and private is essential to the theological task of which we have been speaking. God is not simply one to be talked about, but one to talk to and listen to. Knowledge of God is not just abstract or objective or philosophical, but direct and personal. You get to know a person by communicating, by conversation. You may have to accommodate what you communicate to the limitations of the person with whom you try to communicate, say in the case of someone who is handicapped, but nevertheless you receive and give in a personal interchange. Some communication between persons may not need to be verbalized – words may be too limiting. Yet reflection about a relationship will usually involve some kind of attempt to put into words what it means. Conversation with God is analogous. Our capacity to receive what he has to communicate may limit what he can reveal of himself – and the Christian gospel affirms that he is the kind of God who has accommodated himself to our human capacity in Jesus Christ. There may be occasions when communication will be a bit like lovers holding hands, and verbalization seems intrusive. Yet if the relationship is to grow, it cannot stop there. As far as we possibly can, we need to articulate our response. That articulation needs to be theologically appropriate, and our theology needs to be informed by the conversation. Praying is both the simplest and the hardest part of the theological task. Without it theology is barren.

There are some who claim that theology is a second order activity. It is an attempt to systematize and comprehend the language and truths of faith. Spirituality and theological thinking are distinct. People often contrast critical and devotional use of the Bible, as if you could leave one behind when you engage in the other. Theology is seen as a form of intellectual mastery, an

Addressing God 107

activity that engages one in solving problems or highlighting difficulties, the sort of mental attitute that is incompatible with the humble passive receptivity expected in true prayer. Often the head and the heart are polarized. Increasingly people seem to be turning to sub-rational techniques (though they would probably prefer to designate them super-rational!) to achieve a prayer state that is different from ordinary experience, some to forms of Eastern meditation, many to charismatic speaking in tongues. This climate of thought means that our suggestion that theology and prayer are interdependent will probably not meet with immediate consent. In reaction to the so-called arid analytical intellectualism of European culture, there is increasing denigration of the rational, and most believers would decry any suggestion that you cannot pray without some theological awareness. Some theologians would hesitate to use as material for theology the untestable and supposedly private communication involved in prayer. There is apparently an unbridgable gulf between thinking and praying.

But thinking and praying belong together. Recently I heard of a budding lay preacher who had lost his faith and withdrawn. His faith had begun in an experience which suggested that God had rescued him from death. It had developed in a devotional atmosphere in which it was assumed that it was always God's will to bless. His idea of God never progressed beyond seeing him as a kind of benevolent magician. So when things went wrong in his life, he became an atheist. He simply assumed that since his prayers were not answered, there could not be a God. Mature faith requires all the intelligent understanding we can muster. So does faithful praying. Praying should provide an ever-broadening perspective which is less and less self-concerned and more and more confident, trusting and God-centred, thus providing the sure ground which produces the fruit of loyalty and faithfulness against the odds. It should thus deepen theological awareness, and that awareness should preclude the kind of faith which melts away at the first difficulty.

Praying and thinking belong together. People are ready enough to agree that action belongs to prayer and prayer stimulates action – indeed I have heard it said that one should not pray for anything unless one intends to do something about it. This seems to restrict intercession in a quite unacceptable way, and to imply unfortunate assumptions about the limits of God's activity. But certainly the idea that one can escape responsibility for doing anything about a particular situation by praying instead, needs to be challenged. We may well be the answer to our own prayer if we are sufficiently sensitive and committed. Prayer and action do belong together. But it is not so easy to see how prayer and thinking are related. As already noted, people tend to associate prayer with subjective feelings, passive receptivity and humble obedience, whereas we associate thinking with uninvolved objectivity, problem-solving or critical questioning. The two attitudes seem utterly incompatible. But could this not be one reason why church services and quiet times seem so hopelessly discontinuous with the rest of our lives? For everyday living involves coping with things by planning and problem-solving, thinking and decision-making – even if it is only deciding what to cook for Dad's tea.

Have we mistaken the character of prayer? Does praying involve the adoption of purely passive attitudes? Do we just receive directions? Perhaps our internal debates about what to do should be seen as a form of prayer, arguing the pros and cons in the presence of God, since it is his will we seek to do. Perhaps the whole of the circuit meeting or the church council should be understood as prayer, not just those pious devotional moments at the start. It might transform our decision-making if it were seen in terms of taking responsibility for the world in the presence of God and under his judgment. It might transform our prayer if it were seen not as a way of petitioning for revelation or help, but as entering into a relationship in which part of the responsibility for decision-making rests with us, and that together with God we are involved in creating the future, both individually, and as a community.

If prayer cannot be divorced from the activity of action, how much less can it be separated from the activity of thinking! How often we say to each other, 'Think before you act', or, 'Think before you speak'. Should we not give God respect enough to think before and as we pray? Without constantly expanding thought, prayer tends to become a conventional routine following familiar tram-lines. Without mental concentration, it sinks into a meaningless ritual – vain repetitions. Without critical reflection, it easily becomes idolatry. Without the input of knowledge outside

Addressing God

ourselves, it rapidly becomes narcissistic – an emotional self-indulgence or even self-delusion.

Of course repetitions may have their place in prayer – they are sometimes the only way of expressing what has to be expressed, as in the Hallelujah chorus. Lovers whisper sweet repetitive nothings, and similarly one might sometimes repeat a mantra-like devotional phrase in a meaningful way. Praying familiar liturgical prayers or using the prayers of the Bible, especially the psalms and the Lord's prayer, need not be a conventional routine: such prayers may give us a language in which to pray which goes far beyond our own resources, and familiarity may bring deepened understanding and awareness. Nor should we denigrate the spontaneous in prayer, or those occasions when praying reaches beyond words – when praise is released in tongues or in silence because what needs to be expressed cannot be tied down to inadequate verbal expression. But given all that, it still remains true that concentration of the mind and will upon God is essential to prayer, and so praying and thinking belong together.

Praying begins in adoration, and adoration means to use the imagination so as to fill our minds with a God worth adoring. Most things we adore, we see or hear, taste or feel – we appreciate them with our senses. God we cannot appreciate through the senses, except insofar as he is mediated to us through other experiences. We may get a feeling of adoration, but the feeling is not God. The feeling is our response to something about God which we can know and think about. Imaginative thinking is therefore central to adoration, which involves the re-living of experiences of God, whether our own, other people's or experiences in the Bible, together with the picturing of God's past and continuing activity, and of his fundamental characteristics. This needs to be a corporate activity in which knowledge and insights are pooled. It may happen through group or congregational participation. It may happen through reading, an activity which opens the individual's eyes to wider horizons.

So the knowledge we acquire through science feeds our wonder and joy in creation, our sense of what the God of creation is like, and how he should be adored. The sense of history and of personal story that we gain through reading about the past and reading creative literature feeds our awareness of the richness of human life which has its source in God, and its development through conscious or unconscious relationship with him. Everything we have discussed in this book is relevant to adoration, because it all contributes to our sense of God. Perhaps this is especially true of the reflective theology of the Christian past. It is a great pity that the doctrine of the Trinity is so often seen as a restrictive dogma meaningful only to the intellectual few, instead of a rich and inexhaustible well of meaning which stretches the imagination and deepens devotion, as it is in the traditions of Eastern spirituality. Imaginative thinking is central to adoration. Yet experience may be delusive, imagination misleading, and pictures, even mental pictures, cannot help being inadequate when it comes to God, and therefore to some extent idolatrous. Imaginative thinking has to be refined by criticism, and the sort of critical thinking that ultimately reduces God to an abstraction or a nonentity, has to be counterbalanced by responsible use of the imagination. Both are activities of the mind, and both are essential to appropriate adoration.

We have stressed the importance of imagination a number of times in this book. But perhaps it is necessary to defend the notion that imagination is an activity of the mind. So many seem to restrict rational and intellectual activity to arid analysis and criticism, and see it as inevitably destructive. This is the legacy of the long struggle in the West to banish fantasy from our understanding of the world, a struggle which has often seemed inherently hostile to religion and of its very nature to be sceptical. Let us not underestimate the real benefits of this 'enlightenment', its important contribution to the de-mystification of the universe, its liberating effects upon human consciousness. We are better off for putting superstition in its place, and unmasking it for what it really is. But it has had the effect of distorting our awareness of what rationality involves. Whatever we actually do when we think, our consciousness of what we are doing is bound to be affected by current models, and current models at the popular level are unfortunately limited and blind to certain crucial elements involved.

So a number of people have recently been suggesting that Western scientific culture has a fundamental defect, namely that it is over-analytical, logical, abstract and quantitative in its approach to knowing and thinking, or to put it another way – too rational and masculine. We need to rediscover, it is said, the

Addressing God

synthetic, the imaginative, the poetic, the feminine, the spiritual, and to re-establish its respectability. So for example, in a book called *The Marriage of East and West*, Bede Griffiths, drawing on Jungian psychology, says:

> Every human being is both masculine and feminine . . . In the West today the masculine aspect, the rational, active, aggressive power of mind is dominant, while in the East, the feminine aspect, the intuitive, passive, sympathetic power of mind is dominant. The future of the world depends on the 'marriage' of these two minds, the conscious and the unconscious, the rational and the intuitive, the active and the passive.

Others have associated all this with the discovery that the brain has two halves which carry out these divergent functions – logic, maths, reasoning on the left, imagination, feeling, intuition on the right. The left side, they suggest, has been overdeveloped at the expense of the right, though in a normal healthy person the two necessarily interact in a very complex way. Thus Walter Wink in *Transforming Bible Study* associates this 'split' in the brain with the divorce between academic study of the Bible using the critical intellect, and that imaginative and meditative response to biblical stories which creatively associates them with the real struggles of life. The scientific and analytical has become too dominant in our culture, he suggests, and restoring the balance is essential to the formation of persons.

At first sight this perhaps seems very illuminating, though like all generalizations it soon breaks down. It entirely ignores the tremendous value placed in our culture on the creative arts, music and drama in particular, and it underestimates the extent to which vast numbers of people in the West have remained entirely immune to this 'mathematical' culture, apart from using its products with very little understanding of how they work. But more than that, it caricatures the intellectual procedures of science and criticism, and fails to take account of the close relationship in all intellectual activity between the activities of the left and right brain. Let us explore these points a little further.

It may well be true that science at the school or technician level has had this kind of deadening mechanical effect upon people's minds. We have already said something about the misconceptions of science that poor science education has produced. But any scientist worth his salt knows that intuitive ideas and imaginative analogies play an enormous role in scientific thinking. Of course the new idea has to be tested by critical or experimental techniques, but analysis and imagination function together – both sides of the brain are involved in any new discovery, because the sudden inspired association of two things not seen together before lies at the basis of the new perception and theory. Not for nothing did Arthur Koestler associate the mental processes which produce a good joke, a poem and a major scientific discovery. All depend on seeing one thing in terms of another, on unexpected insight.

It is not science as such that has caused the divorce. Too logical an approach to scientific research can blinker the researcher. The solid unimaginative worker can work away for years without the problem being solved, even though the data may be assembled. It takes the genius to spot what it is all about and what conclusions are to be drawn. Similarly it is not historical criticism which has deadened and distanced the Bible – it is a distortion of it which gets hung up on establishing the facts instead of using linguistic and critical techniques to release the spirit of the text. The latter is what has happened when the methods have been handled by masters.

Another popular misconception is that the thinking process is an individual activity. This again has been reinforced by our educational traditions which stress individual achievement and originality. But scientific research is far from individual. The discussion process, the way one researcher builds upon the work of another, the team-work in many major scientific projects gives the lie to this assumption. The genius referred to in the last paragraph is dependent upon the scientific community, and could not make any contribution without backup and interaction. Thinking requires the stimulus of others to stretch the mind and the imagination.

Imagination is essential to creative work of all kinds. But critical faculties have an important role to play in facilitating the imagination. In the curriculum of philosophical education which developed in the Platonic tradition, the study of mathematics and analytical methods paved the way for theology. By critical and discursive reasoning, the mind was purified and prepared to make the imaginative leap by which intuitive knowledge of God was possible. Stripped of the misleading and the inadequate,

Addressing God

stripped of delusory 'passions' and distractions, the intellect could grasp the ultimate One behind and beyond all things. As this tradition was married with the biblical vision, the critical or negative method was embraced as the way to avoid idolatry, the way of acknowledging the fundamental transcendence of God, the fact that 'no one can see God and live'; and the imaginative or analogical method was embraced as the way to claim positively the wealth of suggestive yet anthropomorphic imagery of biblical language about God. This was a rational way to knowledge of God.

The problem for theology today is that most people have imbibed the false understanding of the thinking process exposed above. As a result we seem to have lost the possibility of regarding knowledge of God as something that belongs properly to a community, and as a rational process with respectable intellectual credentials. The destructive powers of criticism have been let rip. But Descartes showed that radical doubt reduces the basis of knowledge to an absurd nothingness. Being realistic and commonsensical we have to acknowledge that the thinking process has to begin with the simple acceptance of the reality of something. That amount of 'faith' is at the basis of all knowledge. We also have to admit that imagination and insight are vital intellectual faculties, not an artistic extra with slightly dubious credentials, and that our faith is not just a private or individual matter, but a community product, and a public matter.

If we can do this, then we no longer have to resort to that unsatisfactory apologetic ploy that suggests that we know God with our hearts and not our heads. By 'heart' the Biblical writers meant that part of the human person which we would call the mind and will. Of course our feelings must be involved – they are in a sense the powerhouse that drives us to action. But our feelings should not lead us by the nose. Rather our commitment must be a commitment of the whole person, and our understanding must be open to receive the criticism and stimulus of everyone else in the community. Imagination must be refined and tested by criticism, and criticism must be tempered by imaginative realism, so that our minds are engaged – whether we are interpreting a biblical text, deciding what course of action to take, or trying to pray.

Praying means thinking about God so that we can adore him.

Praying means knowing God so that we can fear and love him. Praying means knowing about God and his ways so that we can thank him and address appropriate requests to him. Praying means being able to see ourselves as God sees us – it is not just knowing but being known. Only in the light of this kind of knowledge is proper confession possible – confession is not just wallowing in guilt-feelings, an inherently self-centred and disabling activity; it is allowing ourselves to be measured by the standard of Christ, and being able to face the truth because we trust in the mercy of God. Praying is being admitted to the counsels of God, understanding his will and purpose, and identifying our will and purpose with his. At the heart of Christianity is the revelation of God's *logos*, his word, his mind, embodied in Jesus Christ. Prayer means creative engagement with the meaning that has been revealed. Emotional and meditative states are no substitute for such intelligent and informed engagement. The involvement of the Spirit on both sides of the dialogue, does not mean that we can abdicate responsibility for what is done in prayer. Praying means hard thinking, hard thinking that we do together. (You may like to read the following passages in the light of this paragraph: John 1.1–18; Rom. 8; I Cor. 2.6–16; 13 (especially v.12); and 14.)

Of course feelings are involved. Feelings are involved in thinking about and knowing a human person – even more in addressing that person. Feelings are involved in reading a book or listening to a piece of music. But so is the mind. To be carried away by one's feelings and make a disastrous marriage is a misuse of the capacities for thinking and making judgments which we have been given. To be carried away by one's feelings in listening to good music is to miss half of what is there – knowledge of form and harmony and background (in other words, of the history and criticism of music) enhances appreciation rather than destroying it. To be carried away by a book and not consider whether what is said is right, is to be wide open to exploitation by propaganda. On the other hand, to be coolly rational in deciding who to marry is to lose everything, and you can never completely eliminate the element of risk, or the need to have faith in the other person in a way that goes beyond objective assessment. Similarly analysis of a book or a symphony may be mechanical and dull. These are examples of what goes wrong when only half the mind is used.

Addressing God

To respond fully means the integration of imagination and judgment, of both sides of the brain. Just as appreciation of music may be enhanced by a little knowledge, so may literature and art. Even our response to natural beauty is enhanced by awareness informed by a little geological, biological or ecological knowledge. Not for nothing is Adam given the task of naming the birds and beasts in the creation story of Genesis 2: naming is the way to distinguish, and so to recognize and observe things in their particularity – it is not just the beginning of language but the beginning of science, and it is essential to art. Of course, feelings are involved in our response, but feelings informed by the intellect, imagination tempered by reflection, mind and heart engaged together. That is what creates an appropriate response, whether it be one of appreciation, or action. To adopt a cause implies a commitment made with more of oneself than the logical side of the brain, but if it is not going to go horribly wrong, it must allow that side of the brain to inform it, if necessary temper it, certainly to channel and direct it intelligently. So must the advice and collaboration of others.

All this is also true of praying. Prayer is the concentration of the whole person on God, and the integration of all our faculties, including our thinking, is necessary for the kind of praying which transcends the routine of set pieces or the waywardness of our self-centred interests. It is also necessary if prayer is to be able to inspire action in the world and make judgments upon it under God.

The sudden inspiration or insight, the idea that leaps into focus as we relax and dream or allow our minds to wander, is not to be seen as alien to this process – for that is often how the mind of the scientist has hit upon the answer to the problem that was bugging him. But such thought-flashes do not come out of the blue – they are fostered by study, by reflection, by the enquiry that precedes, and by our interaction with others pursuing the same interests. They would not happen without all this; and not all such thought-flashes are useful or constructive or inspired – it is through the wrestling debate that follows that their conformity with God's will or truth will be recognized or tested. That is what is involved in the work of prayer, and that is why prayer cannot be reduced to saying prayers, or practising meditation. True prayer involves the whole person and the whole of life; it requires concentration of the mind, and the involvement of others.

This need for mental concentration or attention in prayer is brought out most strongly in an essay by Simone Weil on the usefulness of school studies. Without totally concentrated attention we can neither pray properly, nor help people properly, is her view. That kind of concentration is trained through doing mathematical problems and learning languages. The contribution of intellectual discipline can never be underestimated. It is when we are wholly engaged in trying to understand something or express something adequately that we lose consciousness of ourselves and are completely focused on what we are doing. That full engagement is what is needed in prayer and pastoral work – paying attention to the other, totally and without remainder.

If we imagine that Simone Weil meant some kind of mystical contemplation, I think we shall probably be mistaken. The sort of problems you work through, involve focusing on the process of argument; attending to people means listening to what they are trying to communicate with every available faculty and without distraction. The Fathers of the Church used to argue that you cannot know God 'in his essence' but only in his activities, and this distinction can perhaps help us. To attend to another person is to watch what they do, to discern their needs, desires, feelings, worries, hopes, fears, passions, personality, 'essence' mediated through their words, their facial expressions, their actions. We can hardly claim to grasp the 'essence' of another person except in this mediated form. We see what the other person chooses to reveal about themselves, but there are likely to be broad acres of a person's internal life that remain undisclosed. On the other hand, this communication is an important part of what that other person is. In fact, people are often quite different with different people, because the relationship stimulates different reactions and personality traits, and observers usually see things in another person of which that person is unconscious, but which actions and attitudes betray.

Now this analogy must not be pressed too far – I doubt if God lacks self-knowledge in the way we do! But I think it illuminates what the Fathers said about knowledge of God. It is by focusing on his actions that we come to know him, being caught up in his story with the whole of our attention. It is concentrating on this sacred memory, the story from creation, through history, to Christ and on into the life of the church in every generation. This it is which is the burden of the church's liturgy and which provides the pattern of the Christian year. It is by paying attention to this that our minds are fed, and the possibility of new insight into the activity of God in the world around us, in our generation, is prepared. Personal prayer is not discontinuous with this. If it is, it is in danger of losing its bearings. Praying is plugging ourselves into something much bigger than our own personal battery. It is being linked with a vast network, the power mains of the Spirit. The lines run back into the past and forward into the future, as well as all over the world. The outcome is what we discern of God's activities, and that is what we celebrate and participate in. The concentration of prayer begins in paying attention to the story of God, and becoming part of the community which cherishes that memory.

So it is that science, the Bible, the Christian tradition, history and literature all play a vital part in nurturing that appreciation which issues in prayer. They enable concentration of the mind on God. They put us in the right perspective. They furnish us with a language in which to pray. They provide the signposts for decision-making. They contribute to the resources we need to be creative in our praying and our actions. We cannot reflect on God in a vacuum, nor can we praise him, thank him, love him, respond to him, make requests to him or seek to follow his will without his word (*logos* or mind) informing and stimulating our words (minds). Praying and thinking belong together.

Yet for all that it is extremely difficult to consummate the marriage of praying and thinking. Critical thinking goes on in the study, prayer in the chapel and the poor relation, imagination, is consigned to leisure activities or dealing with people. That is the way we see it, and it is hard to undo that brain-washing. Inability to relate them is deepened by sheer lack of interest in doing so, sheer failure to appreciate that they belong together. But even where this is not the case, we experience difficulty in bringing together two apparently incompatible activities and attitudes. Personally I never arrive, but go on travelling hopefully – and that I guess is what the Christian pilgrimage has ever been and will ever remain – a never-ending ascent in which over each crest mounted appears a new summit to be scaled. I have no idea what it would mean to arrive or to be successful in prayer, and I am never satisfied. But the pursuit of personal ends, the constant taking of one's spiritual temperature, the utilization of prayer as a means of escaping problems and tensions and discovering greater health and personal fulfilment – all such attitudes increasinly seem to me to lead to bankruptcy. As individuals we enter into the prayer of the whole church, and to do that we need to think the thoughts of the whole church.

The object of prayer is to be totally focused on God, and that is impossible without deeper and deeper immersion in the hard work of theological thinking. Love and joy are not to be commanded, and usually do not come if they are desperately sought. But against a backcloth of ongoing enquiry and constant expectancy, they come as a glorious surprise, a gift of grace descending out of the blue, never in the same place or the same wrapping as the last one came, but imparting a delight very similar to the delight of solving a problem, or hitting on the exactly the right colour for a particular brush stroke, or exactly the right note for a particular harmony, or exactly the right word for a particular line of poetry. When something is dead right, then everything comes into perspective, and the joy is overwhelming. Prayer is endeavouring to get the focus on God dead right.

There are two contexts in which I have caught a glimmering of what it would mean to get praying and thinking integrated. The first is a very individual one, namely, my attempts to write poetry. Poetry, like prayer, attempts to express things difficult or impossible to express in ordinary everyday language, and this is done by stretching language, by oblique reference or parable or simile, by imagery, allegory and other devices which might be described as 'mediatory'. Like prayer, poetry only lives when there is an undercurrent of feeling, emotional involvement and commitment; yet the structure of the text depends on precise discipline and attention to form – nothing happens by accident. To try and write poetry is to be disabused very rapidly of the idea that the poetic is somehow not as true or much more vague that scientific prose. Poetry has a disciplined precision which average prose entirely lacks. Precisely the right word has to be found, and that aspect of composition may be a cause of intense mental concentration; the critical faculty is at work in accepting or rejecting each imaginative suggestion. In other words the process is a rational one.

On the other hand, the initial thrust of a particular poem is always an inspired guess – a spontaneous idea or image, an odd concatenation of words, a kind of vision which sees one familiar thing in terms of another, so that strange new light is brought to bear upon it. This will be followed, however, by a lengthy process of playing around with it on the back of old envelopes in spare minutes; or by a day's hard work, a mental effort to put the matter precisely and appropriately into the perfectly right language and form. Writing poetry is like problem-solving, and yet it is like praying. Perhaps here we have some clue to what it might mean to concentrate on God, and get praying and thinking integrated.

Writing poetry gives a taste of what it means to find the 'joy of control' in expression. That neat phrase I have borrowed from some programme notes about a Haydn symphony. Control is what gives form to the spontaneous and no great art or literature or music lacks attention to form. There is no such things a 'pure' spontaneous expression. Could concentration in prayer mean paying as careful attention to what we say to God and think about him as we would in wording the most significant letter of our lives? Could it mean refusing to be slip-shod in the way we express ourselves, searching for accuracy and form as well as spontaneity? If praying and thinking are to come together, perhaps it is necessary to pray privately in whatever way it is that we work with maximum concentration – in which case for me, it would mean praying with a pen in my hand, or sitting at the word-processor! Not that I do very often – but there is no problem with wandering thoughts when the mind is actively engaged in finding the right word to say exactly the right thing at exactly the right stage in the thinking process.

The second context bears upon what has been said about the corporate and community dimension in thinking and praying. It is preparing to preach and lead worship. Preaching is not exactly praying, yet it should function as prayerful theological thinking – thinking about God and his word in an affirmative way. The context in worship may seem to preclude negative critical statements, but should not entirely, since the critical approach may be necessary to purify concepts, banish idolatry and bring things under the judgment of God. But the role of that critical process is to make affirmation possible, and the role of affirmation is to elicit from the congregation a prayerful and actively committed response. It is here that theology is most itself, informed by insight and imaginative vision, even if disciplined by analysis behind the scenes. Preaching is the most appropriate form of theological discourse, and it provides the blocks of marble from which prayer is sculpted. How important it is that the preparation for preaching and praying be part of the same process! In preparing for public worship, I have made the greatest strides both in thinking theologically and in learning to pray. It is so important to get it dead right. So often we don't. But when we do, the power released can be awe-inspiring.

Preparing for public worship helps us to grasp both the proper seriousness of preparing to pray, the discipline and thought required, and also how the roots of Christian prayer can only take strong hold in the soil of the Christian community. Private prayer depends upon public prayer. Public prayer is formed out of the wisdom of the whole community. The wisdom of the whole community grows through private prayer. All is dependent upon the network we have spoken of already, stretching from one congregation to another, from one generation to another, back into the past, round about us in all directions in the present, and forward into the future. No one is on their own in this business.

Community praying is where we learn to pray, and if that prayer is poor, the praying of every member will be poor. If that praying is rich, every member will be stretched to greater spiritual maturity, and the riches will overflow into the lives of all. The most demanding and rewarding aspect of the minister's task is to nurture a community in which rich prayer can happen, for every member including himself/herself. It can only happen when the community is involved together with maximum concentration and involvement. This does not necessarily mean lots of 'performers'. An audience may be completely caught up in a compelling performance of say, Elgar's *Dream of Gerontius*, and that is a deeper form of participation than actually contributing rather lamely to the singing. However, one would hope that deep and involved congregational praying would facilitate more and more people to be able to give voice to the prayer of the community, and for the whole to become an explicitly corporate activity. But this can only happen when the focus is on God, and all are moving forward on the road towards him.

None of this means that praying is not also so simple that it can be done by a child. Each is capable of relating to God in his or her own way. The greatest intellectual among the Fathers of the Church was proud of the fact that Christianity could transform the lives of even the simplest – unlike philosophy which could only touch the elite. God is closer than our own breathing, and to speak with him is as natural – or would be if it were not for our own limitations. The greatest possible challenge is to say the Lord's prayer with maximum concentration – many a night I have failed. But the effort to do so bore fruit: the high point of my ordination service was the Lord's prayer – the prayer that links us with the church throughout the world and throughout the ages, the prayer which is both the simplest and the most profound articulation of all we need to express.

All that God asks of us, is that the whole of ourselves be focused upon him. The task of ministry is to facilitate that focus.

Postscript – a poem and a prayer

What is it to pray with faith?
Is it being a bumble bee
 buzzing around the flowers
 sipping the nectar voraciously
 never doubting supply
  supply from flowers, bright flowers?

What is it to meditate?
Is it being a blade of grass
 half-submerged in mud
 beside a puddled footpath
 struggling for light and life
  struggling through mud, thick mud?

What is it to make a response?
Is it being a conjurer's monkey
 trained to perform certain tricks
 trapped in a regular rut
 habit and brain-washed routine
  brain-washed for tricks, neat tricks?

What is discipleship?
Is it being a knitting needle
 wound in a web of wool
 busily used by somebody
 weaving fate's garment inevitably
  weaving with wool, soft wool?

What does submission mean?
Is it being a creature frantic

    caught in a huntsman's snare
    fighting and struggling for freedom
    tighter yet bound in the twine
        bound in the snare, cruel snare?

What is it to contemplate?
Is it being a speck of dust
    caught in a beam of light
    carried on currents of air
    floating with myriads of specks
        floating in light, bright light?

No – the dance of the dust in the light
        and the tool of the mighty knitter
        the struggle of grass for new life
        and the thirst of the bee for nectar
are trapped in passive dependency.
        The hare and the drone will fly free
        and the monkey leap up in the air
        when thinking creates novelty
        when vision makes logic aware.
When the mind takes responsibility,
then there's growth in dependent maturity.

To what shall we liken prayer with faith?
Why – to an explosion
        from submersion
        to conversion!
    The mud's still there
    and so's the snare –
        evil and sin
        hem us in.
But there's transformation
        by fascination
        with exploration
        through concentration.

To what shall we liken meditation?
Why – to an elision
        of precision
        and of vision!
    For the critical

Postscript – a poem and a prayer

    refines the mystical,
    and analysis
    purges synthesis.
So there's integration
    of computation
    with imagination
    and inspiration.

To what shall we liken contemplation?
Why – to enlightenment
    through engagement
    and amazement!
  For pondering
  means wondering,
    and effort's prize
    sheer grace provides.
So there's purification
    from frustration
    and mere sensation
    for adoration.

To what shall we liken obedience?
Why – to an emergence
    to transcendence
    through reverence!
  A committed will
  enhances skill,
    while assurance
    makes for competence
And re-orientation
    to creation
    as oblation
    and celebration.

To what shall we liken our response?
Why – to an identity
    of activity
    and passivity!
  For liberty
  weds slavery,
    and ability

> adopts humility,
> and masculine
> embraces feminine.
> So there's exuberance
> in God's abundance,
> illumination
> and exultation
> With salvation's
> intoxication.

God, I know you as my Father and my lover, and I thank you. I love you and adore you, and my heart is full of gratitude for all you have done for me, for all you are to me.
And yet I know that my perception and experience is limited. I know that my thinking is incapable of responding to you adequately. I am overwhelmed at the enormity of what it means to pray and and think properly. I am ashamed of the idolatry into which I so easily sink, for my presumption, making you in my own image, making you meet my needs, limiting you to my fancies. It is to a projection of my own imagination that I pray. Where is the reality?

Hallowed be thy name . . .
But you are the un-nameable. For how can the incomprehensible be defined by a name? A name spoken is an idol.
Your name is hallowed by silence.
Yet no – how can praise be silent?
Praise seizes on signs, cyphers, substitutes, mediations, images. Yet praise rises above the language it uses and the images it gazes upon. The mind grasps you by a kind of intuition, the unknown, the mysterious, yet all-compelling reality – GOD – and love settles like a glow in the heart.

Knowledge isn't a feeling.
Knowledge isn't dry facts.
Knowledge isn't achievement.
Knowledge is awareness of true relations, proper proportions – the utter nonentity of myself before you, the incapacity of human thinking, your otherness, your independence of my recognition of you, my perception of you, my worship of you . . .
and the crazy mind-blowing necessity of acknowledging my

Postscript – a poem and a prayer

unique importance to you, my responsibility to the truth, my ability to get to know and to create, the essential role of criticism in refining concepts, distinguishing truth from falsity, saving the soul from idolatry, from worshipping a projection of the self.

Hallowed be thy name . . .
Hallowed be the true God – for the true God is not unknown.
Well – unknown in yourself, withdrawn, elusive, greater than we can comprehend, infinite, beyond our grasp – YES
But your glory lies not in transcendence or aloofness, nor is it dependent upon the human glorification of your name. Your glory shines out in your works and your deeds, the signs and symbols and mediators by which you accommodate yourself to our limitations. We do not give you glory. You give glory to us.
Your name be praised, O God.

God, I know you as my brother and my friend, as the one who shares in the pain of the world, bears it, transfigures it.
You reveal yourself to me in human life.

Because of Jesus I can recognize the marks of your presence in the world I know, the ordinary everyday things. Because of Jesus I can perceive your judgment upon the distortions of human worship and love – its hypocrisy and self concern. Because of Jesus I can recognize real goodness, I can discern the true marks of greatness – courage to die in the face of evil and falsehood, love prepared to make the ultimate sacrifice, power to turn evil into good, sorrow into joy, pain into exultation, longing into fulfilment.

Blessed are they who hunger and thirst.
Blessed are they who mourn.
Blessed are they who are persecuted.
Victory within evil. Your name be praised, O Christ.

But how I let you down all the time! The loyalty you demand is more than I can muster. How can I live up to it? What if the ultimate sacrifice were asked of me?

God, I know you as one full of mercy and compassion, as one who has loved me beyond all I deserve. The wonder of your love surpasses all telling, all understanding. Yet what else can I think about! You do not turn me away, for all my weakness, my shame, my disloyalty. Though I forget you, you do not forget me. Though I've cursed you, you have not cursed me. Though I hurt you, though I damage you, you still ask me to serve you. As my brother you stand for me, alongside me; you know and understand my inadequacy, my sense of failure, my forsaken-ness.

And not mine alone – but that of the whole world, the whole sad, travailing world. Sometimes it seems as if you call your people to share with you in being the exposed nerve of humanity, to perceive and bear the judgment and the pain, in prayer, in action, in suffering, in thinking, in being.

Yes, brother, friend, Saviour – take upon yourself the strains and ambiguities, the tragedy of life
    here (in this specific home)
    and here (in that specific situation)
    and here (in that specific relationship).
Take upon yourself the sorrow of this (specific) bereavement, and that (specific) disappointment.
Take upon yourself the boredom of this (named) prisoner,
    the guilt and fear of that (named) person,
    the helplessness of that (named) oppressed community.
Hold in love all your servants who in your name endeavour to bring transformation in society, in individuals, in the world.

God, I know you as transformer within, as the Spirit of love and fellowship in the body of Christ, as the one who prays with me and within me.
I know you as the one who testifies through people to the life and work of Christ, as the one who inspired the witness of the scriptures, and inspires the preaching of the word.
I know you as the one who meets me in other people, whether they are aware of it or not.
I know you as a wind impelling me in unexpected directions, as long as I'm willing to let go, and use my energies in the right direction.

How can I ever praise you and love you enough?
How can I ever learn enough of your ways to recognize the movement of your Spirit? It is so easy to overlook goodness, to

be blind to the wrongs in oneself, in society. Yet things do happen. People do wake up and respond creatively. Slavery was abolished. Penicillin was discovered. Thanks be to you, O God.

Show me how to test the spirits, to discriminate genuine injustice from selfish grievance, genuine religious experience from dangerous hallucination, real change from political fashion, real need from resentment and hypochondria.

Show me how to interpret properly, to distinguish truth from hearsay, evangelism from propaganda, and appropriate judgment from unjustifiable criticism.

Take up my critical faculties, purify them of intellectual arrogance, and use them to release your word from the chains of the past, from bondage to the letter. Use them to release my prayer from narrow self-projection, to release my mind from self-delusion, so that where your Spirit is, there my heart and mind may be, so that my worship may take the wings of the imagination and reach the gates of heaven, the whole of me intensely concentrated on you, totally engaged by your love, so that my life and my actions may be shaped by your will and purpose, and YOU may be ALL in ALL.

Amen

SUGGESTIONS FOR FURTHER READING

Chapter 1: The Implications of Vocation

Eric James, *Stewards of the Mysteries of God*, DLT 1979.
Daniel T Jenkins. *The Gift of Ministry*, Faber & Faber 1947.
Michael Ramsey, *The Christian Priest Today*, SPCK 1985, rev. ed.

Chapter 2: Using the Bible as a Theological Resource

James Barr, *Explorations in Theology 7; The Scope and Authority of the Bible*, SCM Press 1980.
John Barton, *Reading the Old Testament*, DLT 1984.
David Ford and Frances Young, *The Glory of God*, SPCK 1987.
Michael Wadsworth (ed.), *Ways of Reading the Bible*, Harvester Press Sussex 1981.

Chapter 3: Using the Tradition as a Theological Resource

To sample the Fathers, try:

Peter Brown, *Augustine*, Faber & Faber 1967.
J.W. Trigg, *Origen*, SCM Press 1985.

To explore John Wesley, use:

Albert C. Outler (ed.), *John Wesley*, Oxford University Press 1964. A selection of original material for a library of Protestant Thought.

Albert C. Outler, *Evangelism in the Wesleyan Spirit*, Abingdon 1971.

The Reformation is of particular significance for the Methodist tradition, as is Anglican history. But it is impossible to do more than urge people to find other sources of bibliography in a field so wide.

Chapter 4: Using Science as a Theological Resource

Loren R. Graham, *Between Science and Values*, Columbia University Press 1981. A judicious discussion of issues raised for social questions of developments in the history of twentieth century science.

John Gribbin, *Genesis*, The origins of Man and the Universe, Dent 1981. An intelligent and illuminating statement of the present views, eminently readable by the non-scientist.

Konrad Lorenz, *On Aggression*, University Paperbacks 1967. A particular issue is explored here with wide range of evidence and careful analysis. Is man naturally and inevitably aggressive?

Ashley Montague (ed.), *Science and Creationism*, Oxford University Press, 1984. A sensitive but clear rebuttal of the nonsense of 'Scientific Creationism'.

James D. Watson, *Double Helix*, Penguin 1970. If you haven't read it, you should. A vivid account of the discovery of DNA.

Chris Wiltsher, *Everyday Science, Everyday God*, Epworth Press 1986.

Chapter 5: Using History as a Theological Resource

I.R. Christie, *Stress and Stability in late Eighteenth Century Britain*, Oxford University Press 1984. Why was there no revolution in Britain?

J. McManners, *Death and the Enlightenment*, Oxford University Press 1981. An important and illuminating account of changing attitudes to death and dying in eighteenth century France. The volume concerns both Christians and unbelievers.

J.J. Scarisbrick, *The Reformation of the English People*, Blackwell 1984. An elegant account of the unwillingness with which the majority of English people accepted the Reformation and its implications.

David Vincent, *Bread, Knowledge and Freedom*, Methuen 1981. The nineteenth century saw a huge industry of working-class writing; this volume concerns working class autobiography.

M.J. Wiener, *English Culture and the Decline of the Industrial Spirit*, Cambridge Universtiy Press 1981. We are declining as an industrial power because we are losing a substantial portion of our industrial base. But have we ever enjoyed the industrial image of ourselves?

Chapter 6: Using Literature as a Theological Resource

Roland Barthes, *The Pleasure of the Text*, Hill and Wang 1975.
Douglas Brown, *The Poetry of George Herbert*, Hutchinson 1960.
Raymond Brown, *The Gospel according to St John*, Chapman 1971 (2 vols).
Frank Kermode, *The Genesis of Secrecy: On the Interpretation of Narrative*, Harvard 1979. How is meaning revealed, and concealed?
Lionel Trilling, *Sincerity and Authenticity*, Oxford University Press 1972.

Chapter 7: Community Wisdom

J. Hick, *Evil and the God of Love*, Macmillan Second edition 1977, Fontana 1968.
Edwin Muir, Autobiography, Hogarth 1968.
Stewart R. Sutherland, *Atheism and the Rejection of God*, Blackwell 1977.
J.N., Ward, *The Use of Praying*, Epworth Press 1967.
H.A. Williams, *Poverty, Chastity and Obedience*, Mitchell Beazley 1975.

Chapter 8: Addressing God

Mark Gibbard, *Prayer and Contemplation*, Mowbray 1976.
D.W. Hardy and D.F. Ford, *Jubilate: Theology in Praise*, DLT 1984.
Arthur Koestler, *The Act of Creation*, Hutchinson 1964, Pan 1970.
Geoffrey Wainwright, *Doxology: The Praise of God in Worship, Doctrine and Life*, Epworth Press 1980.
Simone Weil, 'Reflections on the Right Use of School Studies with a view to the love of God', *Waiting on God*, Fontana 1959, pp. 66–76.

www.ingramcontent.com/pod-product-compliance
Lightning Source LLC
Chambersburg PA
CBHW072154160426
43197CB00012B/2379